THE MOONS OF PARADISE

The Moons of Paradise

*Some reflections on the appearance
of the female breast in art . . .*

By

MERVYN LEVY

THE CITADEL PRESS
New York

FIRST AMERICAN EDITION 1965

PUBLISHED BY THE CITADEL PRESS
222 PARK AVENUE SOUTH, NEW YORK 3, N. Y.
COPYRIGHT © 1962 BY MERVYN LEVY
LIBRARY OF CONGRESS CATALOGUE CARD NUMBER 64-18241
MANUFACTURED IN THE UNITED STATES OF AMERICA

CONTENTS

Introduction

ACKNOWLEDGEMENTS

Plates 29, 30, 32, 33, 39, 40, 42, 44, 46, 48, 51, 79, 80 are reproduced by kind permission of the Trustees of the National Gallery. Plates 75, 76, 77, by kind permission of the Trustees of the National Portrait Gallery. Plates 3, 4, 6, 9, 10, 23 and 24 by kind permission of the Trustees of the British Museum. Plates 1, 14, 19, 47, 64, 66, 92 and 100 by kind permission of the Musée du Louvre, Paris. Plate 35 by kind permission of the Künsthalle, Bremen. Plate 34 by courtesy of the Musée Bonnat, Bayonne. Plate 45 by courtesy of Palazzo Pitti, Florence. Plate 49 by courtesy of the Museum of Natural History, Vienna. Plate 50 by courtesy of the Borghese Gallery, Rome. Plate 73 by courtesy of the Rodin Museum, Paris (copyright S.P.A.D.E.M. Paris, 1962). Plates 87 (copyright S.P.A.D.E.M. Paris, 1962) and 95 by courtesy of the Museum of Modern Art, New York. Plate 93 by courtesy of the Musée du l'Art Moderne, Paris. Plate 36 by courtesy of the Cathedral, Orvieto. Plate 37 by courtesy of the Sistine Chapel, Vatican Palace. Plate 53 by courtesy of the Staedel Institute, Frankfurt. Plate 55 by courtesy of the Künsthistoriches Museum, Vienna. Plate 61 by courtesy of the Musée de Luxembourg. Plate 62 by courtesy of the Trustees of the Wallace Collection. Plates 63, 85, 89 and 99 by courtesy of the Trustees of the Tate Gallery (Plates 89 and 99 copyright S.P.A.D.E.M., Paris, 1962). Plate 81 by courtesy of the Trustees of Nottingham Castle Collection. Plates 83 and 84 by courtesy of the Musée des Beaux-Arts, Zurich. Plate 86 by courtesy of the Bibliothèque Nationale, Paris. Plates 2 and 13 by courtesy of the Museo Nazionale della Terme, Rome. Plate 96 by courtesy of the Albi Museum. Plate 5 by courtesy of the Museum Olympia. Plate 8 by courtesy of the Ashmolean Museum, Oxford. Plate 12 by courtesy of the Acropolis, Athens. Plate 16 by courtesy of the Bodleian Library, Oxford (M.S. Ouseley Museum Add. 171b, folio 3 verso). Plates 18, 38, 41 and 56 by courtesy of the Uffizi, Florence. Plate 26 by courtesy of the Condé Museum, Chantilly. Plate 78 by courtesy of the Courtauld Institute. Plate 98 by courtesy of the Stedelijk Museum, Amsterdam. Plates 7 and 43 by courtesy of the Prado, Madrid. Plate 11 by courtesy of the Vatican Museum, Rome. Plate 15 by courtesy of the Metropolitan Museum of Art, New York (Gift of John D. Rockefeller, Jnr., 1932). Plate 17 by courtesy of the Church of the Carmine, Florence. Plates 22, 25, 27 and 65 by courtesy of the Victoria & Albert Museum (Crown Copyright). Plates 20 and 21 are from 'L'Art Amoureux des

ACKNOWLEDGEMENTS

Indes' and appear by courtesy of Editions Guilde du Livre et Clarefontaine. Plate 28 by courtesy of the Bamberg Museum. Plate 31 by courtesy of the Germanisches National Museum, Nürnberg. Plate 74 by courtesy of the Trustees of the Chatsworth Settlement.

Plates 88, 90 and 97 (copyright S.P.A.D.E.M., Paris, 1962). Plate 91 is in the collection of the Artist (photo copyright S.P.A.D.E.M., Paris, 1962).

Photographic Sources: Mansell, Plates 1, 4, 7, 18, 19, 30, 32, 39, 51, 66, 67, 75, 76, 101. Mansell-Alinari, 5, 11, 12, 17, 36, 37, 38, 41, 56, 61. Mansell-Anderson, 2, 13, 43, 45, 50, 52. Mansell-Giraudon, 14, 26, 47, 64, 92. Mansell-Bulloz, 100. Mansell-Wolfrum, 55. Archives Photographiques, 34, 93.

ADDENDA FOR AMERICAN EDITION

For plates 73, 87, 88, 89, 90, 91, 97, 99, credit line should read © S.P.A.D.E.M. 1964 by French Reproductions Rights, Inc., New York.

For plate 95, credit line should read Collection, The Museum of Modern Art, New York; Gift of Mrs. David M. Levy.

For plate 98, credit line should read Association Pour La Diffusion Des Arts Graphiques et Plastiques, Paris.

LIST OF ILLUSTRATIONS

INTRODUCTION

Women are like mountains; it is their form rather than their age, or their place in history that commands our interest. They exist, out of time, and it is only the interpretations which men in their lust, or hatred, or tenderness, have superimposed upon the plain reality of the female body that constricts the sex within the compass of an essentially masculine stream of historic events. The aesthetic approach of the Greeks, the misogyny of the middle ages, the hypocrisy of the Victorians have all, in their time, construed the meaning of a woman's body in terms of a prevailing philosophy. In practical terms this means ignoring the reality for the sake of an idea. The real woman has so often been lost in the forests of myth and hatred; neutralized by idealism, or oversweetened by romantic illusion. Perhaps only the Hindu, approaching the landscape of a woman's body in the belief that the mingling of lovers in the act of *mithuna* is the point at which we may achieve union with the divine, has accepted the meaning of womankind for what it is. Only in this conception is the idea subservient to the reality. The essence of Hindu erotic philosophy is the translation of an intellectual-mystical concept into the timeless and placeless terms of sensual joy, or *kama*. The form of the mountains is what matters, not what the ideas of men, laden with conceits, may seek to make of them; beyond their reality.

A woman stands apart from the turbulent stream of events; she is involved in history only in so far as men compel her to assume a variety of fictional roles. Heroine or witch, angel or demon, goddess or whore, she wears the masks men fashion to hide her true face. Against this double concept of woman as the changeless, yet ever changing image of man's desires and hatreds, joys, and sorrows, and madnesses, we must measure the nature of her place in man's world.

It has always seemed to me that nothing in art more potently expresses the reality and the fiction of woman's place in the patterns of human affairs and events, than the portrayal of her breasts by painters and sculptors. The range of aesthetic and sensual interpretation accorded this single aspect of the female nude is so varied and complex, so profound and revealing, that I have thought it sufficiently striking and rich a subject for the book which follows. If I had any doubts at the outset that I would find enough material for a full-length, illustrated work on the subject of the female breast in art, I have since realized that there is material here, not simply for one, but for ten, perhaps twenty books. The more intimately I have searched the provinces of art, literature, and philosophy, the more I have realized the immense potency of the image of the breast. As a visual symbol it is as dynamic and telling as the phallus or the cross, and infinitely more variable and subtle in its diversity of appearances. The golden apples of the classic mould, the great moons of the bosoms of the women in Indian erotic art, or the shrivelled protuberances of the Gothic conception, each in their way express the entirety of a way of life.

My cross references to literature and philosophy, to fable and religion, have only helped to strengthen my conviction that there is no image of muliebrity which more securely enslaves the imagination of men, than that of the breast. It is the pillow of paradise, the cacti of the desert, the point of departure, and the haven of return. For the sculptors of Greece and the painters of the Renaissance it was a perfection less sensual than aesthetic; for the artists of the French Court a delectable erotic toy; in the pattern of Diderot's anti-clericalism it is a symbol of bitter frustration, and for Rouault in his pictures of prostitutes, the personification of decay and martyrdom.

What follows is not a history of the breast in art, nor a chronological survey of its changing appearances in the mirrors of painting and sculpture. I have chosen rather a selection of those historical periods whose character and significance is most intimately revealed in the aesthetic representation of the breast. Here and there the peak of an individual vision rises above the level of a common convention, and some of these intensely personal conceptions of the breast I have woven into the structure of my general landscape. The outsiders, Fuseli, Picasso, and Rouault for instance, are among those artists whose vision of the female breast sets them apart.

And if, as I suspect, the obsessions of man are his measure, then nowhere is his nature more intimately and truly revealed than in the variety of obsessions, all of them passionate, that he has known for women. So often these are focused in the image of the breast. As a symbol of all that a woman can be, in reality or imagination, in fact or in dreams, the breast is a major aesthetic and psychological obsession of the artist and the poet. Let them speak for all. A man's sense of the beauty of a woman's breast can carry him as close to the divine as he might hope to aspire in this world. A wanderer among the hills of her body, he may lose for a while the ferocious egotism from which spring all the ruins of history. And at night, on the breast of the beloved he may shed for a handful of hours the lusts for conquest and for progress that destroy as surely as they seem to build. Only then, in the lost hours, adrift on the shoreless oceans of passion and sleep, will he know the wonder and the magnificence of a woman's body for what it is; a mountain range, standing outside of time, like the snow-capped peaks of Calvi, under whose towering silences I write this introductory note, lying as I would, in the shadow of a woman's breasts, secure and snug in the knowledge that the egocentricities of history are the province of man, and too small a concern either for the attention of women, or of mountains . . . .

CALVI,
    CORSICA
                                   MAY, 1961

For Marie
Under whose breasts
My branches flow
With stars
And my night
Sheds its leaves . . .

1

The Classic Mould

As a reward I hold two apples in my hand,
which grew as twin-fruit from a single trunk.
Nonnos, *Dionysiaca. c.* A.D. 400

When Phryne the Athenian courtesan of legendary beauty was
brought before the Court of Justice and accused of profaning the
Eleusinian mysteries,[1] her defender, Hypereides, had only to tear
open her dress and reveal to the Court the beauty of her breasts.
The Judges, overwhelmed by the loveliness of her bosom, could
not bring themselves to condemn her. And did not Menelaus
when Helen bared 'the apples of her bosom'[2] after the conquest
of Troy, lay aside his sword, and forgive her adultery? A burning
adoration of the female breast is reflected through all the patterns
of Greek art and literature. The exquisite line of the Greek
draughtsman pursues its seductive contours; the hand of the
sculptor thaws its firm apples, warm and living, from the cold
marble.

Yet even in these few introductory observations, a curious,
and paradoxical, note has been struck. The classic ideal of small,
firm, apple-like breasts, would seem quite inconsistent with the

[1] At a Festival of Eleusis, Phryne is reported as having laid aside her garments,
let down her hair, and, in full sight of the people, stepped naked into the sea. One
of her lovers, the sculptor Praxiteles is believed to have used Phryne as a model for
his Cnidian Venus. (Plate 11.).

[2] When Lysistrata unfolds her plan to stop the war between Athens and Sparta
by getting the women of Greece to refuse sexual relations with their men-folk until
the conflict is ended, Lampito, the Spartan, observes: 'It sounds plausible. They say
that Menelaus threw his sword away when he saw Helen's naked breast.' (The
Lysistrata of Aristophanes. From a translation by Louis Untermeyer.)

boisterous and voluptuous accounts which describe in Greek—
and relevant Roman—literature, the revels and loves of the gods
and their companions. In spite of all this, there is an evident
timidity in the approach to the breast which suggests that while
it was often the flashpoint of desire, it was also, for some reason,
an awe-inspiring, and restraining influence even on the most
rampaging, and lustful of gods and satyrs. It is only with the
greatest reserve and discretion that Dionysus 'brings his loving
hand near the breast of the girl standing before him and,
apparently by accident, touches the prominent roundness of her
dress' (*Dionysiaca*).

Indeed, one wonders if, in spite of their arrogant swaggerings,
the gods and satyrs of ancient mythology were very successful in
their pursuit of women after all. Nymphs and Naiads were frequently chased—and sometimes caught—by the wild revellers
who stalked the pipe-mad glades of Arcadia in drunken bands,
but their rewards were often pitifully meagre. Nonnos, the Roman
poet whose *Dionysiaca* describes in great detail the personal
history of the god of wine, relates one such incident. The occasion
is a drunken ramble by Dionysus and a gang of satyrs.

> 'Near the fountains, another (satyr) driven by the insane
> impulse of drunken excitement, chased a naiad of the
> waters; he would have seized her with hairy hand as
> she swam, but she gave him the slip . . . Many of the
> horned satyrs joined furiously in the festive dancing
> with sportive steps. One felt within him a new hot mad-
> ness, the guide to love, and threw a hairy arm round
> a Bacchanal girl's waist. One shaken by the madness of
> mind-crazing drink laid hold of the girdle of a modest
> unwedded maid, and as she would have no love-making
> pulled her back by the dress and touched her rosy thighs
> from behind. Another dragged back a struggling mystic
> maiden while kindling the torch for the god's nightly
> dances, laid timid fingers upon her bosom and pressed
> the swelling circle of her firm breast.'

The gestures of the satyrs are surprisingly restrained and the
women hardly co-operative, while the breast is treated with something of a schoolboy's respect for strong drink. The satyrs were
not apparently very accomplished lovers and even great Zeus
himself was not above resorting to unsporting tricks in order to
realize his desires. Did not the cad change himself into a gentle

dragon of many coils so that he might 'ravish the maidenhood of unwedded Persephoneia' (Nonnos) whom he had earlier spied upon while she bathed.

> 'She loosed the modest bodice which held her breast so tight, and moistened her skin with a refreshing bath, floating in the cool running stream . . . But she could not escape the all-seeing eye of Zeus. He gazed at the whole body of Persephoneia, uncovered in her bath.'
> (Nonnos)

A trifle unbecoming, one would think, that the top god should need to resort to such a low subterfuge, but indicative again of that lack of finesse which so often distinguishes the amorous pursuits of the gods and their companions. There were of course many conquests, but one is struck by the overall melancholy of their love longings, and by their strange faint-heartedness in the presence of the 'little apples' of the female breast. Why? Is it that the gods after all were uncertain in which direction their desires really lay? A powerful thread of homosexuality linked the sexual patterns of Greek society and, since the gods were created in the image of man, it is perhaps not surprising that the paederasty and tribadism commonly practised by the Greeks should be favoured by their deities. In the heterosexual culture of ancient India the breast appears as a heavy and dominant element in the artist's conception of woman. In Greece, the contrary operates. Everywhere the emphasis is upon the 'apple ideal'.

> 'The silver-footed maiden was bathing, letting the water fall on the golden apples of her breast, smooth like curdled milk.'   (Rufinus, *The Greek Anthology*)

The boyishness of this ideal, particularly when combined, as in so many statues of the female figure, with a pronounced masculinity of conception—thick waists and highly developed muscles—suggests the prevailing influence of the homosexual cult upon the shaping of aesthetic conventions. The *Dionysiaca* is laced with homosexual incident, notably the passion of Dionysus for the boy Ampelos. In Book X, Nonnos describes a frolic between the god and the boy.

> 'While Bacchos lay willingly on the ground the boy sat across his naked belly, and Bacchos in delight lay stretched at full length on the ground sustaining the sweet burden on his paunch.'

Such passions are likely to neutralize, or to weaken at least, the natural and confident flow of man's desire for woman. Sexually, the gods of the Greeks found themselves on the horns of a melancholy dilemma: a sad question of 'which way shall I turn me?' So we have the hesitance and uncertainty of both Dionysus and Zeus in many of their heterosexual leanings. But the gods, poor devils, were only the carnival image of man himself. It can be argued from all accounts that the dominant note in the erotic life of ancient Greece was that of male homosexuality, and the gods had little choice but to follow suit. Women were loved, and married, of course, but the great passions of writers like Pindar, Anacreon, Solon, Theognis and Alcaeus were reserved for boys.

Inevitably, the aesthetic conventions of the period were shaped in the gymnasium rather than the bed-chamber. In sculpture, the form of the female breast is modified by the homosexual approach. The art forms of Greece evolved from a society in which paederasty was widely practised, and while there are many ostensibly 'feminine' interpretations of the female figure by the sculptors and draughtsmen of Greece, these are usually combined with a muscularity and a masculinity that suggest a male, rather than a female emphasis of interest.

Many of the depictions of Greek maidens that appear in pottery and vase painting are distinguished by a slender boyishness of figure. Here again the emphasis is upon male qualities. (Plate 10).

And since the patterns of history sometimes repeat themselves, it is interesting to reflect that the same thing happens, though for different reasons, in the fashions of the nineteen-twenties. The obliteration of the natural form of the breast, the evolution of the flat-chested look, and the general craze for boyishness and masculinity among women that succeeded the mother cult of the First World War, and the matriarchal obsessions of the Edwardian era, locked neatly into the rise of the emancipation movement, and the clamour of women for equal rights with men.

A line of T. S. Eliot will perhaps best summarize the character of the classic mould.

> *Uncorseted, her friendly bust gives promise of pneumatic bliss.*

Firm and resilient, not soft and yielding forms. A pillow for a soldier's rather than a voluptuary's rest. The ideal is well expressed in a fragment of Philodemus from *The Greek Anthology*:

'Charito has completed sixty years, but still the mass of
her dark hair is as it was, and still upheld by no encircling
band those marble cones of her bosom stand firm.'

Yet the tribadism prevalent in Lesbos and Sparta must certainly
have played a part in shaping the conception of the classic mould,
though more obliquely, and as an abstract influence perhaps,
since perversion among Grecian women was apparently less common than among men, and presumably more localized. Nevertheless it complicated sexual patterns and contributed its own share
in the shaping of an aesthetic 'middle sex'. The hermaphrodite
image is common in Greek art. (Plate 3).

From the island of Lesbos, the home of Sappho, the practice
of 'Lesbian love' gradually emerged and took roots among the
women of the Greek mainland. More than three centuries after
the death of the poetess the practice of tribadism was solidly
established as a common feature of sexual life and 'to play the
Lesbian' is a phrase that occurs frequently in the plays of
Aristophanes.

Not all the references to heterosexual love in Greek literature
can ever neutralize the mood of dual-sexuality that riddles the
erotic life of her society. It is a strain which leads to the melancholy
splitting of personality that is so much a part of the dilemma of
homosexuality. Categorically, it leads also to a subtle schizophrenia
in the arts.

Horace called Sappho 'the male', and from what we can gather
of her love for the maiden Atthis she appears to have been the
dominant partner, though torn at the same time by a tender
melancholy, typical of a woman loved, and then abandoned. It is
in this vein that she writes:

> The moon and Pleiades have set, midnight is nigh,
> The time is passing, passing, yet alone I lie.

It is generally believed now that Atthis eventually separated
from Sappho to live in faraway Lydia. The poetess writes to a
mutual friend: 'Among the women of Lydia she shines, as the
moon surpasses the stars in brightness when it rises over the
sea . . .'

★

A clearer picture of the complexity which the dual-sexuality
of the Greeks created can be gathered from the *Dionysiaca*. This

Roman reconstruction of the Greek myths summarizes at many points the intrinsic dilemma of sexual duality. Once again we are reminded of the fact that the gods and goddesses of Greek mythology were created in the likeness of man, and with all his failings intact. The following extract from the *Dionysiaca* describes a scene between Artemis, the virgin huntress, and her handmaiden, Aura. The goddess, standing on a river bank is wringing out her dripping hair. Aura, who has also been swimming, joins her mistress on the bank. She criticizes the softness of her breasts, and the general femininity of her body.

> '. . . your rounded breasts are full and soft, a woman's breasts . . . not a man's like Athena. I ask pardon of your beauty, but I am much better than you. See what a vigorous body I have! Look at Aura's body like a boy's, and her step swifter than Zephyros! See the muscles upon my arms, look at my breasts, round and unripe, not like a woman. You might almost say that yours are swelling with drops of milk! Why are your arms so tender, why are your breasts not round[1] like Aura's to tell the world themselves of unviolated maidenhood?'

Aura, herself a virgin, has implied that the soft womanliness of Artemis's figure and flesh are abhorrent. A true virgin should be boyish, with firm breasts, and a lithe, masculine physique. The idea of assessing female beauty in masculine terms is yet another manifestation of the dual-sexuality from which the aesthetic conventions of Greek art are forged. Artemis is naturally incensed by Aura's stinging criticism, and unburdens herself to Nemesis, at one time a woodland deity.

> 'Virgin all-vanquishing, guide of creation, Zeus pesters me not, nor Niobe, nor bold Otos; no Tityos has dragged at the long robes of my Leto; no new son of earth like Orion forces me: no, it is that sour virgin ·Aura, the daughter of Lelantos, who mocks me and offends me with rude words . . . I am ashamed to describe her calumny of my body and her abuse of my breasts.'

The comment on Zeus, although incidental, is interesting. He is recognized as a bounder and a tormentor of women. Out of sympathy for Artemis, Nemesis conspires with Eros to rob Aura of her virginity. The method is typically brutish. Eros makes

[1] Like 'apples'?

Dionysos mad with lust for the young virgin who is then tricked into drunkenness, and finally ravished by the god while she is asleep. A characteristically caddish piece of treachery.

★

One other factor may be taken into account when considering the origins and evolution of the classic mould. The legend of the Amazons, a mythical race of women warriors who combined in their person the strength of the athlete with the beauty of the goddess, provided a popular subject for Greek artists, especially the sculptor. The Amazon image is of course simply a variation of the hermaphrodite theme, in which it is possible for artists to concede the ideal of the 'apple breast' while stressing at the same time the more significant character of the male physique. Amazon women were supposed to have cut, or burnt off one, or even both, of their breasts so that their movements in bending the bow and hurling the javelin should not be hampered. Their dress was the short chiton, with the unmaimed breast usually exposed.

But god or virago, the reflection in the mirrors of art is always that of man. The aesthetic image is the measure of his striving, and the classic mould of the female breast succinctly describes the dilemma of dual-sexuality that tormented, however exquisitely, the Greeks.

It may be of course that this sexual conflict is simply another manifestation of the quest for an ultimate balance and harmony which the Greeks sought in life, and found in art. Harmony, balance, and proportion are the essence of the classical ideal, and it is these qualities that distinguish the sculpture of the golden age. Here is mirrored the most complete and perfect expression of the Greek mind. Their aesthetic ideals were the product of minds liberated from the fears and tyrannies that had prevented, in earlier civilizations, the emergence and growth of free thinking, and the rise of humanism in the arts. As far back even as the Homeric poems this sense of freedom is expressed in the criticism of kings and gods. And indeed why not? The kings, tyrants, and gods of the Greeks were simply men. No man claimed divinity, as did the Pharaohs; man was the measure of all that it was possible for him to be, and from within himself alone did he seek to create the aesthetic standards that expressed his dream of an ultimate perfection. He claimed no supernatural powers, realizing to the full that the proper study of man is man himself, a concept that

25

was echoed with considerable fervour during the Italian Renaissance. The freedom of thought which the Greeks exercised in art, science and philosophy was their great contribution to the evolution of liberal civilization. In this respect they broke with the despotisms and tyrannies of Egyptian and other oriental civilizations, to establish a conception of society in which for the first time man himself was the starting point of all enquiry into the nature and meaning of his place in the universe. It was a quest of the absolute; a search for dispassionate truth. The character of the classic mould—of the appearance of the breast in Greek art—is but one reflection of that quest. The desire to integrate within the aesthetic image the sum of man's highest aspirations, and to reconcile in the same artifact the conflicting elements in his personality, was the goal of classic art. The symbolic image is the point at which all the rivers meet and mingle in the one harmonious fountain of art. This is particularly apparent in the classical face. In the sculpture of the golden age there is no 'male' or 'female' face, only a supreme, sexless, impersonal image of absolute beauty (not necessarily acceptable to us) applicable to both male and female figures. The Greeks sought an aesthetic 'becoming one'; the blending of opposites in a time-less harmony. For them, the images of art were an end. Not so for the civilization of classical India. The Hindu of the Gupta era convened the forms of art largely as a stimulus to those erotic activities through which, in the practice of *Kama* the individual soul could achieve an impersonal union with the infinite. Beyond the forms of art Hinduism sought a spiritual 'becoming one'. This, from our point of view, is the fundamental difference between the active interpretation of the breast in Hindu sculpture, and its relatively passive acceptance in the sculpture of Greece, where sexual conflict finds a point of rest. The 'apple breast' is a compromise between the diametric tuggings of heterosexualism and homosexuality. Harmony is achieved, if not in human conduct, then in the aesthetic image. One cannot of course generalize conclusively in this matter; the 'apple breast' is the ideal. Often, quite naturally, there are departures from this norm. Sometimes the breast is more generously treated as in the voluptuous, swelling globes of the Caryatis from the Erechtheum (Plate 4), or in the full-blown sensuality of the bosom of Aphrodite gaming with Pan (Plate 6). But this is not the shape of the classic mould, or the form of the symbolic image I have discussed.

In their day-to-day affairs the Greeks were beset like other civilizations, before and since, by all those clamorous evils that destroy as fast as men build. Wars, and internal bickerings, and struggles for power and conquest; the paradox of a slave system within the fabric of 'democracy', and the existence of kings and tyrants, were an intrinsic part of their way of life. Yet even so, all was tempered with a humanism and a freedom of thought that were unknown before their time. The search for perfection in philosophy, science, and art particularly, the quest of the absolute —the absolute good, the absolute beauty, the absolute truth— was the measure of their culture. They fought wars continuously, both against would-be invaders of their homeland, and among themselves. Wars that ravaged and laid waste but could not divert their energies from the search for an aesthetic absolute. Our wars are all-embracing; theirs were incidental to the more important issues of art and philosophy. Naturally, for the Greeks, the search was closely bound up with the human figure. This was the pivot of prowess in war and love. The cultivation of muscular strength and of bodily grace were the complementaries of success on the battlefield and in the bed-chamber. So the need was felt to arrive in art at a synthesis of strength and beauty. Hence the continued pursuit for the harmony of an ideal type.

I have talked about the nature of this ideal so far as the female breast is concerned, but it might further illuminate the whole question of the subtle, hermaphrodite synthesis of pure classical sculpture—apple breasts, gracefulness of line, and muscularity—if we examine a little more closely the ideals of Greek life. Here, the pleasure principle was the directing agency, and the body its vehicle of expression. Sensual pleasure as an end in itself and not, as in the practice of the Hindu philosophy of *Kama*, as a means to an end, was a pronounced feature of the Greek outlook. Aristippus (*c.* 435-356 B.C.) founded an entire philosophical school through which to argue that pleasure is the only good in life. It is from his doctrine of pleasure that the term 'hedonism' derives. The omnipotence of sensuality as a prevailing influence in Greek life is everywhere apparent in her history. The voluptuous excesses of Greek kings and tyrants are proverbial. Coupled with ferocious drinking bouts, the life of pleasure for its own sake was pursued religiously by the aristocracy of Greece. Young and beautiful boys figured prominently at their luxurious orgies, and were enjoyed, often openly, along with the courtesans and other women in attendance, at these gay and riotous functions. Homosexuality was practised without shame, and as an intrinsic element in the pursuit of pleasure. This presumably was the background of everyday life in the great days of Athens and, since the society of the period was composed, broadly, of only two classes—'aristocratic citizens' and slaves—it is fair to conjecture that the life of pleasure was the prerogative of all 'free' men.

Heracleides Ponticus, a disciple of Plato, wrote a book on 'Pleasure', many passages of which have been preserved. In this he stresses that the luxurious and voluptuous life is a right reserved for the ruling classes, whereas hard work is the lot of the slave.

★

One fact is now clear. The classical ideal reconciles the polarities of heterosexual and homosexual desire in the symbolic image of woman. Conversely, although this is not our special problem, the soft, voluptuous femininity of many of the male statues produced by Greek sculptors is also evident. (Plate 5).

The sexual life of the Greeks was coloured, perversely, with a powerful strain of homosexuality. No moral criticism is involved here, rightly I think, since the Greeks were civilized enough to regard sex not as a moral issue, but purely as an integral part of the full and happy life. The sexual perversions that complicated, to their disadvantage, the pattern of their society, can be condemned only upon psychological grounds. The moral strictures that arose later in Christian times were of course—and still are— quite untenable because they are based upon the unhealthy, and indeed absurd myth of 'original sin' and the fall from grace. In late medieval art the treatment of the female breast appears superficially to compare with the apple breasts of Greece. But here the smallness of the forms are in themselves a condemnation of sensuality. Like ungathered fruits, withering away, they hang, dry and sexless on the parched crucifix of the body. Even the figures in Hieronymus Bosch's great triptych 'The Garden of Earthly Delights' (Plate 7) are dry twigs. The symbolic eroticism of the central panel is clouded by the phantasmagoria that rises like a madness from the conflict between the lusts of the flesh, and the Christian concept of sin. There is no sensuality here. Not even if one accepts the interpretation of Wilhelm Fränger that the main panel depicts the millennium: a becoming-one-with-god through the gratification of the senses; a paradise regained wherein the whole of creation partakes of an ecstatic celebration.

The image of human nakedness in medieval art is perforce drained of its sensuality.

★

Whenever the breast is frankly and prominently portrayed as an erotic element in painting and sculpture, it often follows that the costume of the period offers liberal opportunities for its appearance in everyday life: either wholly, in *décolletage*, or in such a way that the covering garments while actually concealing the nudity of the breast, deliberately emphasize the voluptuousness of its form. This is as true of the sweater cult of our own time, as it was of the thin, clinging garments, fashionable among Greek women during the Hellenistic Age. Woven from imported cotton and silk into a gauze-like fabric called 'Coan', Theocritus calls them 'wet garments', while later, Lucian must have been speaking of much the same kind of attire when he commented that 'clothes of a tissue as fine as a spider's web are only pretence, so as to prevent the appearance of complete nakedness'.

The erotic possibilities of such apparel were exploited naturally by the *hetairae*, although generally speaking, garments of this kind were commonly worn by many beautiful women. Earlier, in Aegean times, as we can see from the paintings at Knossos in Crete, and from small statuettes of the period, the ladies of the Minoan court, and the serpent priestesses of the island wore long, colourful skirts, and a tight-fitting bodice from which the breasts protruded quite naked (Plate 8). This charming and coquettish fashion clearly shows that while the Cretans must have been familiar with the severe, monumental productions of Egyptian art, they possessed themselves a keen sense of the *joie de vivre*: at least at court level, where the palace painters and designers provided a gay, elegant, and amusing background for the luxurious and exuberant life of the king and his courtiers. The most significant feature of Cretan art is the break it made with the restricted and sombre traditions of Egyptian and Babylonian art to release the aesthetic eye into less stiff and pompous fields of artistic expression. Exuberant colours, and a charming sense of the decorative, freshly expressed, herald the awakening of the liberalism that was developed later in classical art.

But there seems to have been little inclination among Aegean artists to compress the female breast as did the classic mould, with its widely spaced 'golden apples'. On the contrary, the breast was often treated with a buxomness that would have delighted the eye of Rubens or Renoir.

The nudity of the bosom, so fashionable among Cretan women, was much favoured more than two thousand years later in both France and England during the eighteenth century.

★

With the death of Alexander the Great in 323 B.C., the classical age comes to an end and the Hellenistic era opens. Most authorities will agree that this is the point at which the forms of classical art begin to coarsen. Their perfection was gradually dissipated in a slow decadence that was to continue until at last the culture of Greece was absorbed into the far less subtle aesthetic of the Roman Empire.

But whether we think of the Hellenistic Age as one primarily of decline, or rather as a period in which the invigorating influence of classical art was exerted from the limits of Northern India on the one hand, to Alexandria, the centre of Hellenistic civilization, on the other, the era has a special bearing on our immediate study.

With the decay of classicism, paederasty retires more and more into the background, and the influence of women begins to be more strongly felt. They became more conspicuous in public life, for instance, a fact which contrasts sharply with the relatively exclusive domination of the male over the entirety of the classical scene. During the Hellenistic Age there was an increase of intercourse between young men and the *hetairae*, and the general build-up of a normal attitude to the joys of heterosexual love. In *The Greek Anthology*, Dioscorides (2nd century B.C.) writes with a clean, voluptuous fervour, of the passion of man for woman:

> 'They drive me mad, her rosy lips,
> Where from my soul its nectar sips,
> Her eyes a liquid radiance dart,
> Traps to ensnare my fluttering heart,
> Her breasts, twin sisters firmly grown,
> Two hills . . .'

Earlier, the dramatist Chaeremon (*c.* 350/80 B.C.) had painted with exquisite sensuality an evocative vignette of female dancers which subtly captures the mounting tempo of heterosexual desire.

> 'The one lay there, and showed in the moonlight her
> naked breast, after she had thrown her garment off her
> shoulders; another, while dancing, had bared her left

hip, naked in the sight of heaven she offered a living picture; another bared her well rounded arms, while she flung them round the delicate neck of another. One of them exposed her thigh, as the slit in her dress with its folds opened, so that the charm of her radiant body unfolded itself beyond all expectation.'[1]

Written immediately before the opening of the Hellenistic Age, a silver thread of tribadism still delicately flavours the scene, although of far greater interest is the light this passage throws on the male perspective. At the same time it describes the seductive possibilities of the *chiton*. Was it here the short *chiton* traditionally favoured by Spartan women, and slit from waist to knee? (Plate 15). Or the full-length version opening from hip to toe? (Plate 12). Either way the intoxicating sensuality of these clinging garments, now hiding, now exposing the ecstasy of the naked flesh, must indeed have ravished the eye: heightening, even when they concealed the hillocks of the firm breast, their warm voluptuousness.

In Greek sculpture the forms of the breast are often emphasized by these flowing garments, just as in Indian sculpture (Plate 21) the long necklaces of the women endorse the roll and swell of the bosom's ocean.

In the classical age the idealization of the breast was carried into pottery and vase painting, where the figures of the women attired in *chiton* or *peplos* often display the widely spaced apples of the classic mould. The pleated linen *chiton* was commonly worn with the overfold pulled up over the girdle so that the top half clung to the breasts in a sort of tight-fitting blouse. The more voluminous *peplos* was less seductive. (Plate 14).

In fact, of course, the breasts of Greek women, on the average, could have been no less imperfect than those of a twentieth-century housewife, and they sought, as do women today, to rectify, at least superficially, such imperfections as the unsightly hanging of the bosom by wearing beneath the *chiton* a breast-band or bust-supporter, an equivalent of the modern *brassière*. Hans Licht suggests that the breast-band also served 'to limit excessive development of the bosom', and quotes Martial (A.D. 41-104) as saying that 'there may be something for our hand to encompass and cover'. Here again we can trace the influence of the classic mould echoing through into a late period.

The Roman poet Ovid (43 B.C.–A.D. 17), whose witty *Ars*

[1] Hans Licht, *Sexual Life in Ancient Greece*. (Routledge & Kegan Paul.)

Amatoria is as much a picture of the elaborate game of love, as it is a commentary on Roman affairs or the passions of the gods, offers sound advice on the deployment of *brassière* and corset in the Third Book of the *Ars*, sometimes called 'The Ladies' Companion':

> 'If a girl's shoulder look too high
> A *brassière* will downwards force it,
> While lack of flesh she may supply
> By deft adjustment of her corset.'[1]

The Art of Love has been so diversely translated, both into prose and verse, that the choice of an English version is naturally very wide. I have selected those which best suit my own purposes.

Ovid is important to the present study since both the *Ars Amatoria* and the *Remedia Amoris*—the remedies for love—provide, as does the *Kāmasūtra*, not only a technical handbook of the art of love, but a key to the nature of an ideal; that concept of perfection, either spiritual as in ancient India, or physical as in classical Greece, towards which, through the medium of sexual passion, the most profound of man's yearnings is directed. A preoccupation with physical perfection, or with the application of compensatory measures where this is lacking, forms a substantial part of Ovid's advice to women in the third book of the *Ars Amatoria*. All of which suggests a norm. In classical times the apple breast was an integral part of this ideal, and finds an echo in Ovid's talk of 'faultless breasts' (Book Three of *The Art of Love*). The great globes of the breast in Indian erotic sculpture are the antithesis of the classic mould. For the Hindu lover, 'beauty' was a means, not an end, and apart from a general passion for heavy breasts, a slim waist, and broad hips, his requirements would seem to have been far less fastidious than those of the classical lover. The *Kāmasūtra* is never critical of beauty (Ovid was often brilliantly satirical in his enumeration of bodily defects); it classifies the sexes not by standards of physical perfection, but according to the size of genitalia. Men and women are each divided into three size categories, and Vatsyayana pairs off those best suited to extract the maximum of pleasure and fulfilment from the love battle.

Ovid's instructions for the love game are more sophisticated than Vatsyayana's, because the sexual passion he seeks to arouse, and fulfil, is in itself an end; pleasure is all. It has no extension—

[1] F. A. Wright, *The Art of Greece*. (Routledge & Kegan Paul.)

at least not 'officially'—beyond the acts of love. All the possible gratifications of the art of love are restricted by this philosophy to the orbit of sexual pleasure, and these in relation, and ratio, to an inflexible concept of physical beauty. But the ideal of bodily perfection is a hard taskmaster.

Lie on your back, if your face and all of your features are pretty;
  If your posterior's cute, better be seen from behind.
Milanion used to bear Atlanta's legs on his shoulders;
  If you have beautiful legs, let them be lifted like hers.
Little girls do all right if they sit on top, riding horseback;
  Hector's Andromache knew she could not do this: too tall!
Press the couch with your knees and bend your neck backward a
    little,
  If your view, full-length, seems what a lover should crave.
If the breasts and thighs are youthful and lovely to look at,
  Let the man stand and the girl lie on a slant on the bed.
Let your hair come down, in the Laodamian fashion:
  If your belly is lined, better be seen from behind.'[1]

How melancholy that the dream of aesthetic perfection should harbour such a nasty little worm. Love subsists as much upon the imperfections of the beloved as upon her beauty and her graces.

In reality the 'perfect breast' would be the exception rather than the rule, so that the search for aesthetic perfection as the basis of sexual pleasure must be something of a phantom. The depth of cynicism which the pursuit of perfection must inevitably engender is clearly indicated in the *Remedia Amoris* with which Ovid completed his erotic cycle. There is nothing in his work to suggest that love is anything but a game, rooted in the frail flesh, and as transient as a ray of sunshine. The concept of romantic love which was to emerge in the middle-ages is quite outside the scope of his philosophy. Dante would have won little sympathy from Ovid; except for the offering of a remedy for love that is utterly incompatible with the romantic attitude. Imagine such advice as that which follows offered to Dante, or for that matter to Keats. It is most unlikely to have been taken since the essence of romantic passion is the fattening of the imagination on every shade of wretchedness. Separation from the beloved, unrequited adoration, the marriage of the loved one to another, even death itself, all this is the fuel of the romantic ardour. On the other

[1] Ovid—*The Art of Love*. Translated by Rolfe Humphries. (John Calder.)

hand complete possession of the beloved is the death of romantic love. Supposing Keats had married Fanny, or Dante his Beatrice; or supposing they had taken Ovid's advice? What agonies we might have been spared . . .

So now listen to me, young men who have been so deluded,
Whom, for all of your pains, love has completely betrayed.
I have taught you to love—do you want to know how to recover?
Mine is the hand that will bring wounds, and the cure for the wound.[1]

Then follow detailed instructions both for the discouragement of 'the loved one', and for the breeding of personal disenchantment.

When you possibly can, fool yourself, ever so little,
Call those attractions of hers defects, or possibly worse.
If she has full round breasts, call her fat as a pig; if she's slender,
Thin as a rail; if she's dark, black as the ace of spades.
If she has city ways, label her stuck-up and bitchy;
If she is simple and good, call her a hick from the farm.
Whatever talent she lacks, coax and cajole her to use it:
If she hasn't a voice, try to persuade her to sing;
If she trips over her feet make her dance; if her accent's atrocious,
Get her to talk; all thumbs?—call for the zither or lyre.
If she waddles or limps, be sure to take her out walking;
If she has bulging breasts, don't let her wear a brassière.
If her teeth aren't too straight, tell her a comical story;
Make it a sorrowful tale if she has watery eyes.
Sometimes it works very well to surprise her early some morning,
Hardly expecting a call, when she's not fixed for the day.
All of us let ourselves be fooled by a woman's adornments,
Jewels and gold; we see more than there is to the girl.
Sometimes I wonder where, in the midst of all this abundance,
Lies the essence of love, under the shield and disguise.
So, come unforeseen; safe, you will catch her defenceless,
Sorry to see and be seen, victim and failure and fraud.
(Still, it is not too safe to trust this prescription too blindly;
Beauty, artless, naïve, often has power to deceive.)
Go take a look sometime when she's smearing her face with cosmetics—
Don't let a little thing like decency stand in your way—
You will find boxes and things, a thousand different colours,

[1] Ovid—*The Art of Love*. Translated by Rolfe Humphries. (John Calder.)

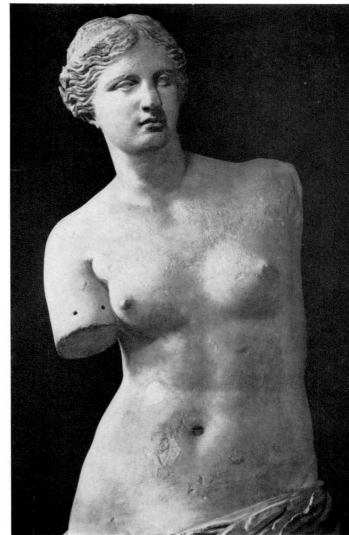

1 Venus de Milo, *c.* 100 BC

2 Venus de Cyrene. Graeco-Roman

3 Hermaphrodite. Graeco-Roman, original *c.* Second century BC

4 Caryatid from the Erech-theum, Athens, *c.* 420-413 BC

5 Hermes of Praxiteles,
c. 350 BC

6 Aphrodite and Pan
Gaming. Incised bronze
mirror-cover. Fourth cen-
tury BC

7 Hieronymus Bosch (active 1488-1516). Detail from the central panel:
The Garden of Earthly Delights

8 Priestess from Knossos. Cretan, *c.* 1600 BC

9 Aphrodite. Graeco-Roman, original *c.* Fourth century BC

10 Pottery painting. Greek, *c.* 510 BC

11 Cnidian Venus. Praxiteles, *c.* 350 BC

12 Mourning Athena, c. 470-460 BC

13 The Birth of Aphrodite. Ionian. Ludovisi Throne. Rome, c. 440-430 BC

14 Procession of Maidens. Frieze
of the Parthenon, *c.* 440 BC

15 Wounded Amazon. Roman
Copy of Greek Work, 440-430 BC

16 Indian Painting. Mogul, *c.* 1700. 'The bowls of her breasts the colour of milk',
Kashmiri Bilhana

17 *above*, Masaccio (*c.* 1401-1428). The Expulsion; 18 *above right*, Botticelli (1444-1510). Detail. The Birth of Venus; 19 *right*, Ingres (1780-1867). La Source

20 *above left*, Khajuraho
(eleventh century). Couple
Embracing; **21** *left*, Kha-
juraho (eleventh century).
Vishnu and Lakshmi; **22**
above, Lovers Embracing.
Ivory. Madura, Madras
State (eighteenth century)

23 Matrika. Detail. South India. Ninth century. 'Her golden necklace was swinging under her naked breasts . . .' (Chandi Das). Thus Krishna pictured Radha in the poet's words; **24** *above right*, Mithuna Group. The Adibuddha Vajradhara in union with his Sakti. Nepal. Seventeenth century

25 Yakshi (from a Jain Stupa). Mathura. Kushan Dynasty. Second century AD

26 Pol de Limbourg (active before 1399 to before 1439).
The Fall. 'Très Riches Heures'

27 Virgin and Child. English. End of twelfth century

28 Eve. Detail from Adam and Eve. Bamberg Cathedral, *c.* 1235

29 Lucas Cranach (1472-1553). The Close of the Silver Age

30 Rogier van der Weyden (1400-1464) Detail. The Last Judgment

31 Hans Baldung (c. 1480-1545). Madonna and Child

32 Robert Campin, Master of Flémalle (*c.* 1378-1444). Virgin and Child

33 Rubens (1577-1640). Detail. War and Peace

34 Dürer (1471-1528). Naked Hausfrau

35 Dürer (1471-1528). Women's Bath

36 Signorelli (*c.* 1441-1523). Detail. The Blessed

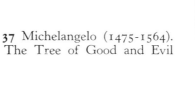

37 Michelangelo (1475-1564).
The Tree of Good and Evil

38 Venus de
Medici. Hellenistic

39 Bronzino (1503-1572). Venus, Cupid, Folly and Time

40 Garofalo (1481-1559).
Amor and Voluptas

41 Lorenzo di Credi
(1459-1537). Venus

42 Bordone (1500-1571).
Daphnis and Chloe

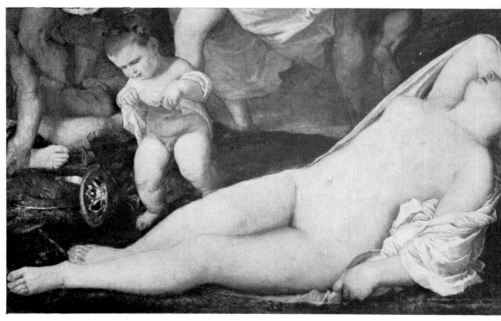

43 Titian (c. 1477-1576). Detail. Bacchanal

44 Mother and Child. Milanese
School. Sixteenth century

45 Titian (*c.* 1477-1576). St
Magdalen

46 Veronese (1528-1
Detail. Respect

47 Manet (1832-18
Blonde with Bare Bre

48 Piero di Cosimo (1462-1521). Fight between Lapiths and Centaurs

49 Venus of Willendorf. Palaeolithic carving. Between 40,000 and 10,000 BC

50 School of Leonardo. Painted about 1505. Copy of a picture now lost

51 Correggio (1494-1534). Venus, Cupid and Mercury

52 Michelangelo (1475-1564). Figure of Night. Tomb of Giuliano de Medici

53 Veneto (active 1502-1535). Portrait of a Courtesan

54 Rouault (1871-1958). Prostitutes

55 Rubens (1577-1640).
Hélène Fourment

56 Titian (c. 1477-1576).
Venus of Urbino

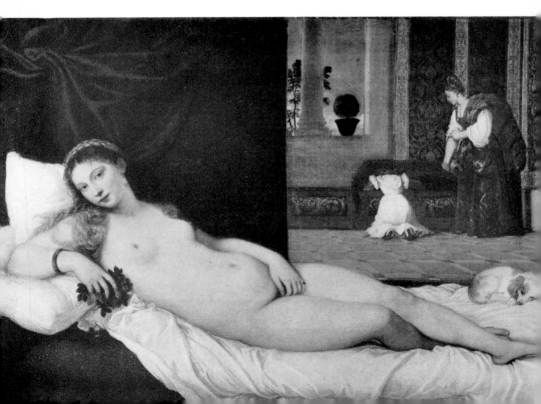

Also lotions and such, dripping all over her chest.
Drugs like these smell worse than the tables the Harpies polluted,
Giving me, more than once, more than an impulse to retch.[1]

Ovid's cynicism, however entertaining, is clearly the death-knell of classicism, just as it is the obverse of the dream of the classic mould. In the flesh, perfection is unobtainable. Once this had been clearly realized the culture of classical Greece had reached the threshold of the Hellenistic decline. Three centuries later Ovid documented the psychological nature of this decay. He saw too deeply into the true nature of things, and while the ideal of physical perfection is implied in the works from which I have quoted, it is now suspect. The realism of his attitude to erotic affairs matches perfectly the naturalism of Hellenistic art, and in this sense he is a true reflection of the decay of the classic ideal. Long before his birth, the golden apples of the classic mould (Plate 13) had swollen into the more probable breasts of the Aphrodite of Melos (Plate 1). A comparison between the earlier goddess (Plate 9) and the later Venus clearly illustrates the dissolution of the classic ideal in Hellenistic art. The latter goddess still wears the hermaphrodite classic face, but the bosom has fattened, while the figure as a whole has coarsened and lost altogether the sylph-like aspect of the girl of the golden age. She is, by comparison, a positive thug, with the physical attributes of a heavy-weight boxer rather than the light-weight grace and charm of her prototypes. Her breasts are those not of the classic mould, but of more human form. The pursuit of hedonism had finally dissipated the classic dream.

Yet even the admirable, if less exalted, naturalism of the Hellenistic Age was to vanish, through Rome, into the swirling mists of the middle ages. A thousand years of darkness, of religious censure and persecution were to veil the glory of the female breast until, with the dawn of the Renaissance, it emerged, tentatively at first, its naked sexuality suitably clad in the double-talk of allegory, mythology, and religion.

Not until Rembrandt painted the body of Saskia for its own sake, was the breast restored to the throne of sensual grace. And with Rembrandt its portrayal assumes a new dimension. For the first time the breast is pictured, not as ideal, or symbol, but as a human reality; as the warm, breathing flesh of a real and particular woman. Meanwhile, in those dark centuries when Europe

---

[1] Ovid—*The Art of Love.* Translated by Rolfe Humphries. (John Calder.)

35

was isolated in the stony wilderness of the middle ages, a great civilization arose in India. Woman, outlawed by Christianity in the West, became the heart-beat of Hindu philosophy and Indian art.

2

The Moons of Paradise

Even today I can see her, her slender arms encircling my neck,
  my breast held tight against her two breasts,
her playful eyes half-closed in ecstasy,
  her dear face drinking mine in a kiss.

*

Even today, if this evening
  I might see my beloved, with eyes like the eyes of a fawn,
with the bowls of her breasts the colour of milk,
  I'd leave the joys of kingship and heaven and final bliss.
> (From the Kashmiri Bilhana: 11th/12th
> centuries)[1]

When a woman is in passion and finds an occasion to bend over her lover, sitting or standing in a secluded place and presses his body with her breast and the man in return takes hold of her in his arms and squeezes her breast on his chest, it is called *The Breast Embrace.*
> (Vatsyayana: Kāmasūtra. *Principles of the*
> *Science of Sexual Passion.* The Hindu Art
> of Love. *c.* 3rd/5th century A.D.)

Indian literature is brilliantly studded with references to the female breast, while almost every branch of her sculpture, from life-size carvings in stone to the most delicate and diminutive pieces of ivory, is bountifully laden with its full, ripe fruit. To understand the true significance of the breast as an element in Indian art, one must first appreciate and understand the meaning of the sexual

[1] *The Wonder that was India.* A. L. Basham. (Sidgwick & Jackson.)

principle in Hindu philosophy. At the core of the *Vedas*, almost certainly the oldest religious text in the world,[1] are the principles of *Dharma* (religious and moral duties), *Artha* (the acquisition of material possessions), *Kama* (desire and pleasure), and *Moksha* (redemption or spiritual salvation through union with the divine). But it is with *Kama* and *Moksha* that we are at present concerned. *Kama* means 'desire', and the pursuit and enjoyment of sexual pleasures through which we may achieve *Moksha*—the becoming one with the great impersonal spirit: union with the divine. Vatsyayana speaks of coital movement and the release of *Atman* (self) in the climax of sexual passion as the most ravishing, powerful, and revealing of all sensual pleasures, and talks of the minor delights of 'kissing, embracing, titillating, etc.' The Hindu philosophy of life is a healthy and a happy one, seeing love and sex as a gateway to the highest forms of spiritual revelation. Within this context it is evident that the female breast has an important part to play both as the source of sensual pleasure, and as a foothill on the road to *Moksha*. But let us look more closely at the whole question of the Hindu conception of the meaning of love, and trace our way from this general consideration to the breast in particular.

The two quotations above form the key to an understanding of the way in which the romantic and practical polarities of love should normally, and naturally, complement and fulfil each other. No philosophy of living other than that of classical Hinduism has either perceived the nature of this complementation, or succeeded, which is even more remarkable by our own decadent standards, in effecting a prophylactic and life-enhancing blending of these apparent extremes.

The romanticism of the Hindu writer and sculptor is distinguished by the fact that it is the transmutation of *the known*, as opposed to the Western custom of imagining *the unknown*, which forms the working basis of Indian romantic and erotic art. To the romantic poet of the West, woman is the unattainable, a shining star beyond reach, while for the Hindu poet the beloved is very much the attainable paradise, here and now; the voluptuous organ of fulfilment. The ghostly damosels of the West wandering like sick lilies to the cry of 'Pity!—love!—aye, love—in pity give me all . . .', have no counterpart in Hindu poetry. Here, as I say, woman is the known, and not the unknown quantity. If the poet would write of the beauties of his beloved it is out of knowledge

[1] A series of more than a thousand hymns composed about 1500 B.C.

and fulfilment that he speaks. The stanzas from the Kashmiri
Bilhana are the most eloquent proof of that, and of the philosophy
of love which made such writing possible. To know, utterly, is
therefore the basis of the extroverted romanticism of Indian art,
while the introverted romanticism of the West stews in the juice
of its blind ignorance. Thus Vatsyayana's elegant and eminently
practical instructions are delightfully echoed in the first of the two
romantic Kashmiri stanzas. The one is the logical complement of
the other, and the sane and balanced romanticism of the poem
reveals the delicate, and relatively slight transmutation from the
plain reality of the beloved's breast, into the exquisite, lyric notion
of 'the bowls of her breasts the colour of milk'. This is the poetry
of fulfilment, of having arrived, of the completeness which distinguishes the whole range of Indian erotic art. The gentle nostalgia
of the stanzas is not a whine, but the echo of a deep consummation.
Western poets are more given to bleating about unrequited love,
or of reading into the natural simplicity of the erotic situation
disfiguring romantic complexities. Swinburne is the great master
of this fault. His is the poetry of defeat. The romance of frustration and disillusion is the key to the malaise of much of our own
love poetry. In the last resort not even Byron could find cause for
rejoicing. 'So we'll go no more a-roving' is a tragic indictment of
the incapacity of the Western psyche to find in love, and its
sensual gratifications, the source of completeness and contentment.
Why the desperate exhaustion of Byron—the wretched mopish-
ness of Keats? Simply because, in the West, the romantic polarity
of love is used, not as the spiritual complement of the practical, but
solely as a vehicle for the venting of frustration and disillusionment.

> *Too late for love, too late for joy,*
> *Too late, too late.*
> *You loitered on the road too long*
> *You trifled at the gate . . .*
>
> (From 'Bride Song')

Christina Rossetti's lament crystallizes the situation perfectly.
It is important to establish this contrast in romantic attitudes,
since we cannot hope to approach the ecstasy and the fulfilment
that lie at the heart of Indian erotic art, from the standpoint of the
sexual malaise which taints our entire culture. The appallingly
inhuman doctrine of 'original sin' is of course the root of this
sickness. For two thousand years love and sex have presented the
Western world with a vast problem. But for the Hindu of

39

Vatsyayana's day there was no problem here; one loved as one breathed—without shame, and just as naturally. In the West on the other hand, where the romantic concept of love is neither balanced nor complemented by the application of practical principles, there arise inevitably those fevered and demented fantasies that form so great a part of our romantic literature. The ravaged visions of Swinburne, the pathetic whining of Keats, and the obscene ravings of Poe are witness enough to the degradation of the romantic concept of love as conceived and expressed by so many of our own poets and writers. The sexual inhibitions that originated with the rise of Christianity are unquestionably the source of the soul sickness which culminated in such nineteenth-century depravities as Swinburne's lunatic babbling about—'hard eyes that grow soft for an hour'—and— 'lips full of lust and of laughter, curled snakes that are fed from my breast'. To say nothing of Ruskin's monstrous maladjustments, which are of course as much symptomatic of the disease of an age, as of the degeneration of a personality.

The technique of pornographic allusion, the masking of sexual truth out of hypocrisy in allegorical and other devices—as in the nude painting of Cabanel, Bouguereau, and many Victorian painters—are phenomena peculiar to the West which, for the past two thousand years, has been unable to think—or act—straight on matters of sex. How refreshing then are the delightfully frank, tender, and evocative references to the charms of the beloved in the Kashmiri Bilhana, and how wholesome and naturally stimulating, the amorous cookery of Vatsyayana.

'With the bowls of her breasts the colour of milk'; what Western poet has ever written more subtly, so purely, or more hauntingly, of the breasts of the beloved? When Keats wrote of Fanny's 'warm, white, lucent, million pleasured breast' it was the stuff of dreams he wrought, not the living flesh of the known beloved. While the mildew of incipient puritanism infects both Lovelace and Habington with their fantasies of the nunnery of the chaste breast.

> Yee blushing virgins happy are
> In the chaste nunnery of her breasts,
> For he'd prophane so chaste a fair,
> Who e'er should call them Cupid's nests.
> ('To Roses in the Bosom of Castara'.
> William Habington: 1605-1654)

★

It is hard for the sexually bankrupt civilization of present-day Europe and America, finally emasculated by the oblique, substitute sexualism of a crudely suggestive cinema, press, and television service, to accept without embarrassment the gloriously frank and pure conception of sexuality that permeates and characterizes so much of the great art of India. For an age that admits the phallus only within the context of Freudian symbolism, as when Mrs Cramp-Saddle dreams repeatedly of being chased by umbrellas—'*Gentlemen's* umbrellas at that doctor!'—the cult of the *lingam*,[1] and the *lingam* worship that are so closely interwoven into the whole fabric of Hindu thought, is a little unnerving. But for countless Hindus of the golden age of Indian art the *lingam*, both as symbol, and as fact, played as significant a part in the daily lives of an immensely humanistic and cultivated people as the cross plays in the life of a pious Christian. As a symbol of joy, and of continuous creation, it is the fountain of all our possibilities as human beings. To deny this is to end as the West has done, on the rough rocks of frustration, and indeed, some might even think of madness. The sexual patterns of Western society today can hardly be called sane. But this is quite consistent with our traditions. For the Christian world the sexual act has never been the centre, the pivot upon which turns the whole of our striving for union with the divine, but only the brutish and intolerable machinery of reproduction. A curse to be suffered. At the heart of this attitude is St Paul's arrogant and inhuman doctrine: 'I would that all men were even as I myself.' Naturally this doctrine is the antithesis of the Hindu philosophy of *Kama*. The concept of the union of essence (*purusa*) and substance (*prakriti*) through coitus (*mithuna*) (Plate 24) has no parallel in the pattern of Christian philosophy. The release of the drop of self (*atman*) into the shining ocean of the infinite, 'the becoming one' through the climax of the act of love, this is the metaphysical basis of *Kama* and the significance of its place in Hindu philosophy. There would seem to be evidence enough that the divinity intended this pattern to operate, but no proof that 'the chastening

[1] The *lingam* (phallus). An emblem in the form of a cylindrical stone topped with a rounded cap. Professor Max-Pol Fouchet writes in *The Erotic Sculpture of India* (Allen & Unwin): 'It symbolizes the creative energy of the male. As a ritual object it is widely venerated and is to be seen not only in temples dedicated to Siva, but also in the streets of towns, by the wayside in country places, and in private dwellings. The faithful have small models just as the devout Catholic has his crucifix; many wear it as a charm. The *lingam* stands on a flat base, the *yoni*, which by its shape—round, oval, polygonal or square—represents the female sex, the matrix. The two are often carved with a realism that cannot be denied, especially the phallus.'

fires' of Christianity have produced on the anvil of abstinence anything but hypocrisy beyond belief, and cruelty beyond redemption. Blake, the visionary Christian, was well aware of this when he wrote:

> *Abstinence sows sand all over*
> *The ruddy limbs and flaming hair,*
> *But desire gratified*
> *Plants fruits of life and beauty there.*

★

The precedent for the concept of *Kama* is of course in life itself. Paul's grudging concession to the flesh—'It is better to marry than to burn'—is monstrously unnatural. Basically, *Kama* means the pursuit of joy and revelation along a road that can be naturally, and happily, travelled by all men. The *Kāmasūtra* sets out to provide both men and women with the technical wherewithal to find their way along this winding road.

The period that concerns us in this short study extends from the beginning of the Gupta era in the fourth century, to the close of the middle ages, when the tides of Muslim tyranny and destruction swept across Northern India. The early traditions of Hindu thought and art were carried right up to the building of the great temples of Khajuraho (10th/11th centuries) and Konarak[1] (13th century). These blistering tributes to the joys of sexual passion, writhing with erotic groups in every conceivable—and inconceivable—state of sensual delight, are without parallel. Their ecstasies range from the bestowal of the most tender and delicate caresses, fluttering like the wings of butterflies about the breasts of the beloved, to engagement in the most vigorous and imaginative acts of coitus. They bring to life all the teachings of the *Kāmasūtra* and display as nowhere else the ecstasy of the female breast. There are of course many references to the breast in Vatsyayana, and these are richly complemented by its appearance in Hindu sculpture where it presents itself as the most voluptuous organ of the female anatomy. Certainly it is meant to inflame the erotic appetites, and to stimulate the practice of Vatsyayana's many recipes for preliminary love play. Apropos the present

---

[1] The temples of Khajuraho, a North Indian village about 100 miles south-east of Jhansi were built during the period A.D. 950 to 1050 under the Candella kings. The largest and finest of these is the temple of Kandariya, dedicated to Siva. At Puri, also in Northern India, stands one of the most famous of all Hindu shrines, the 'Black Pagoda' of Konarak. Dedicated to the sun god Surya, it was built between A.D. 1238 and 1264.

subject his list of kisses include *The Balanced Kiss* (kisses on the curve between the breasts), *The Forcible Kiss* (kisses implanted *on* the breasts), and *The Chaste Kiss* (kisses given from the breasts downwards to the waist). While among his recipes for erotic 'scratching and biting' is *The Boar's Bite*:

> 'the most appropriate portions of the body for this type of biting are the female breasts and shoulders. A small portion of the skin of the breast or shoulder is held between the teeth and chewed, and then another portion is taken, and so on, leaving a long, unbroken line of red stain.'

Commenting on the violence of *The Boar's Bite*, one authority notes in the most charming and matter-of-fact way that for obvious reasons this particular bite should be strictly avoided 'when dealing with virgins or other peoples' wives . . .' I cite these incidental references to the breast because they illustrate the extent to which its overpowering appearance in Hindu sculpture was matched by a complementary obsession in Hindu erotic thought.

It is the easy and frank acceptance of the art of love as an intrinsic element in the day-to-day pattern of the normal, healthy life, which contrasts so strikingly with the sense of shame in sexual matters that springs like a canker from the hell-pit of Christian puritanism. The breast is always proudly, often mischievously, and even wantonly, displayed in Indian sculpture. It bursts like a summer rose from the ripe garden of the exuberant flesh. The difference between this joyous acceptance of the breast by the Indian artist and its morbid rejection by early Christian artists is nowhere more clearly demonstrated than in the convention of covering the breasts with the hand to indicate the shame and disgrace of original sin. The figure of Eve in Masaccio's 'Expulsion from Eden' (Plate 17) is an expression of this attitude. The convention is also employed by Botticelli in 'The Birth of Venus' (Plate 18) where in spite of the ostensible paganism of the subject, it springs from the conflict between the spirit of medieval Christianity and the neo-paganism of the Renaissance. It was a dilemma which tore the soul of this troubled genius.

The prominence given to the breast in Indian sculpture is of course closely related to the type of female most admired by Hindus. She was the woman of heavy breasts, slender waist, and broad hips (Plate 25). The extent to which Hindu sculptors exaggerated these natural characteristics is the prerogative of all romantic art, although, as I have suggested, the basis of Indian erotic romanticism is rooted in fact, rather than imagination, so that its idealizations are boldly extroverted: contrary to the hesitant, 'discreet', and hypocritical idealizations of Western neo-classical styles (Plate 19). But these mannerisms are not to be confused with the idealizations of Greek sculpture itself. Here, the conception of the breast, although in reverse from that of Indian art, is no less fresh and direct. The emphasis as I noted in the previous chapter is usually upon small, constricted forms, a convention which evolved not only, it would seem, from the cult of athleticism, but also from the widespread practice of homo-sexuality

But the sexual life of ancient India was relatively unclouded by perversion, and in singing the praises of the breast the sculptors and poets of India were notably single-minded. They reached unparalleled heights of voluptuousness, often elegant as well as extravagantly forthright. So the poet Chandi Das makes Krishna speak of his beautiful cow girl mistress, Radha:

> 'Her golden necklace was swinging under her naked breasts,
> That pointed like the tips of the hills of Sumeru . . .'

While a descriptive translation in J. J. Meyer's *Sexual Life in Ancient India* (Routledge) is even more evocative:

> 'As she went along, her breasts, scented with a heavenly salve, black-nippled, rubbed with heaven's sandalwood, and shining from her necklace, were shaken up and down . . .'

On the practical side too, Suvarnanabha, another great authority on sexual technique, offers his own recipe for *The Breast Embrace*.

> 'The woman presses her breast on the chest of her lover, throwing the whole weight of her body upon him, so giving great pleasure to the man from the soft touch of her flesh. This embrace is best enjoyed when the couple lie side by side . . .'

To match such exquisite imagery and pleasurable instructions, it is no wonder that Indian sculptors freely indulged their imagina-tion and cut from the stone a dream of the breast that could scarcely find any counterpart in the living flesh. Max-Pol Fouchet's

The Erotic Art of India refers to the sculptor's extension of reality into the idealizations peculiar to Indian erotic art:

'The breasts have no droop, scorning gravity's law. They are spheres, self-enclosed worlds, attached directly sometimes to the torso underneath, as if they were not carried by the torso, but sprang straight from it, or rather as if the fruits of some orchard never spoiled by the hand of time were grafted onto the flesh to assuage man's hunger and thirst and renew them endlessly. Of Parvati it is said: "She bent under the weight of these twin globes, like a fruit tree heavily laden." '

★

One of the most seductive and revealing conventions of Indian sculpture is the way in which the long necklaces of the women undulate over, around, between, and under the breasts, so as to emphasize the beauty and voluptuousness of their form. They flow in caressing streams as tenderly as the playful, meandering fingers of a lover, flickering over the breasts of his beloved in the ecstasy of love-play (Plate 20). Whether the lovers are relaxing (Plate 21), or exploring the innermost throes of *mithuna* (Plate 22), the delicate caressing of the breast which plays so conspicuous a part in the art of love, expresses too, the rhythms and movements of the life force. The hands ripple ceaselessly over the breasts like waves, coaxing the last paroxysms of delight, stripping away the petals of ecstasy one by one, until the heart of the flower is exposed, and the *atman* released into bliss. Hand and breast are therefore often complementary in Indian sculpture, the hand inducing either passion or repose; the eternal cycle of action, and respite from action; the surge and swell of the life force so potently symbolized in the forceful, aggressive thrust of the breasts; the moment of respite from the rhythms of its eternal pressures, so tenderly described in the gentle support which the hand of Vishnu offers the breast of Lakshmi (Plate 21). This charming group reminds one too of the essential morality of the relationship between the sexes in Hindu philosophy, for Lakshmi, the goddess of fortune, was the wife of Vishnu, the Preserver who, with Brahma, the supreme impersonal soul, and Siva, the lord of creation, form the great triad of Hindu gods. She incarnated herself as the spouse and mistress of the incarnations of Vishnu, so that she appears as Sita, the wife of Rama, as Rukmini, the queen of Krishna, and as Radha, his adored cow girl. She is often depicted as a mature woman, as here, in which role her breasts suggest rather the comforts of the wife and mother, than the devouring sensuality of the young mistress.

But the most interesting feature of the relationship between the gods of Hindu mythology and their wives was the idea that the goddess possessed no separate identity from that of her husband. In the form of a *sakti* she was an extension, an emanation of the male, representing his creative energy in female form. So we arrive at the essential monism of the Hindu religion: the idea of oneness which is expressed even in the apparent duality of the sexes. Yet the striving for oneness through *mithuna* is also the source of life—of creation. In his progeny, the devout Hindu symbolizes the splitting of the supreme god, Brahma, into the 'many', through 'desire'. Love represents the complementary, and *moral* striving of the many to regain the blessing of oneness, through the same desire. The foundation of the sex relationship in Hindu life was the family. In the procreation of numerous children the Hindu could express both the manyness, and the oneness, of Brahma. The breast is therefore a symbol both of sensual delights, and of motherly blessings and comforts. The twin fountain of lust, and of maternity, feeding alike the passion of the lover and the hunger of the infant.

'I am the lust that procreates,' Krishna proclaims in the Bhagavad Gita. The female breast is fuel for the fires of this divine lust, and the mingling of *lingam* and *yoni* symbolize the creation of the world, and of human life.

> 'The woman is the fire, her womb the fuel, the invitation
> of a man the smoke. The door is the flame, the entering
> the ember, pleasure the spark. In the fire the gods form
> the offering. From this offering springs forth the child.'
> (*Chandogya Upanishad*)

This then is the philosophical and religious climate from which emerged the conception of the female breast peculiar to Indian art. Both in its forthright voluptuousness, and in the gentle transmutation of its stark sensuality into the tender, lyric romanticism of Hindu erotic poetry, it manifests the most impressive and evocative symbol of the sexual life, second in potency only to that of the *lingam*. The *yoni*, by its very nature, can make little impact as a visual symbol, its significance being more abstract than literal. In short, it is less easy to display or to formalize visually than the phallus or the breast.

46

THE MOONS OF PARADISE

So far we have considered mainly the philosophical background of Indian erotic art; let me now mention some of the chief facts about the social setting of Vatsyayana's time for the *Kāmasūtra* sets the pattern of social and sexual behaviour not only for its contemporary period, but also for the whole of the middle ages in India. Vatsyayana's great work is therefore the mirror of an entire culture, and of inestimable value to the student of the golden and middle ages. During this period—as indeed from the earliest times—sexual activity between husband and wife was looked upon as a religious duty, as well as the source of pleasure and spiritual revelation. So too was the procreation of many children. Nor was the sexual act thought of, as so often in Western history, merely as an outlet for the animal passions of the male. The practice of love as an art was the primary concern of the *Kāmasūtra*, providing as it does, detailed instructions on erotic technique, with a view to ensuring that both partners derive the maximum of pleasure and fulfilment from *Kama*. But this does not mean solely the divine satisfactions of *mithuna* itself. All that subtly, and gradually, leads to the climax of love, is taken into account. The art of wooing the beloved and of winning a wife is fully dealt with by Vatsyayana, from which it is clear that the preliminaries of the art of love as practised by cultivated Hindus were immensely refined, gracious, sweet, and infinitely tender; the feelings and the satisfaction of the woman, in every respect, being of primary importance:

> 'Whenever the sweetheart happens to be washing her lover's feet, he should pinch her fingers between his toes. While giving or receiving anything from her he should mark it with his nails.[1] Whenever they happen to be alone he should get her gradually used to caresses and nail scratching, and he should make a declaration of his desires through gestures and actions. He should on no account speak in a manner that may embarrass or distress her.'

This is merely one of the many charming paragraphs in a work that was, in its time, the indispensable handbook of the cultivated man about town.

The art of conversation too was rated a trump card in the game of love. Vatsyayana records that Ghotakamuka advised: 'Though

[1] The marking of leaves with finger nails or teeth was a recognized method of addressing love appeals to a woman.

a man loves a girl ever so much, he never succeeds in winning her without a great deal of talking.'

But if the *Kāmasūtra* was primarily intended as a handbook for the leisured classes, the sculptures of Khajuraho and Konarak are the living testimony of its influence throughout the general structure of Hindu society over a very long period.

The life and work of the sage Vatsyayana coincided with the golden age of Hinduism and Indian art. The epoch of the Imperial Guptas (A.D. 320-500) was a period of security, of freedom from political troubles and foreign invasions, in which a sophisticated civilization with a strong bias towards humanism, both in its concept of daily life and the nature of its deity, found in the practice of the arts, the mainspring of its culture. The masses and the leisured classes alike were conversant with the arts of music and dancing, which were generally practised as communal activities essential to the well-being of the citizen. As in Greece, the courtesan occupied an honoured position in society, and was expected, at the top level,[1] to be fully trained in the 'Sixty-Four Arts' of the *Kāmasūtra*. Singing, writing, drawing, painting, the 'Making of different kinds of beds for different occasions and purposes'—'Imitation of the sounds of instruments, sweet birds, etc.'—'Training of birds for mock fights and for serving as messengers'—'Skill and dexterity in rubbing and massaging the body and the head, shampooing and dressing the hair'—'The art of scanning and constructing verses'—these are a selection from the 'Sixty-Four Arts' of the *Kāmasūtra*, which includes also a special section for the instruction of prostitutes. This tells them how to conduct their business to the best advantage. So in ancient India, the high-class courtesan occupied a position in society comparable with that enjoyed by the *hetairae* of Greece.

> 'A courtesan of a pleasant disposition, beautiful, and otherwise attractive, who has mastered the arts,[2] has the right to a seat of honour among men. She will be honoured by the king and praised by the learned, and all men will seek her favours and treat her with consideration.' (*Kāmasūtra*)

Indeed the Golden Age of the Guptas can be compared in many ways with the Golden Age of Greece (6th/4th century B.C.). Both

---

[1] Vatsyayana lists nine grades of prostitute, ranging from the Free-lance (*Kumbha dasi*) to the most high ranking, the Courtesan Prostitute (*Ganika*), mistress of 'The Sixty-Four Arts'.

[2] The Sixty-Four Arts.

eras were founded on humanistic concepts, and both, though differently in some respects, accepted the practice of sexual activities as an essential part of the good life.

The esteem accorded the courtesan by civilizations whose achievements in the practice of the arts rank highly—as in Greece and India—suggests that need of intellectual and sexual stimulus beyond the compass of family life, which is felt by all intensely cultivated societies and individuals. Throughout the patterns of both Jewish and Christian society, where the profession of prostitution has been—and still is—looked upon as unnatural and disgraceful, there is a notable decline in the cultural aspirations of the community as a whole. The common prostitute of modern times cannot be compared with the cultivated courtesans of Greece, India, or Renaissance Italy.

The art of India, like that of Greece, was an integral part of a way of life, dependent far less upon individuals than the social and religious concepts that bound indivisibly together the society and its culture. An expression of the esteem in which Hindu society held the prostitute can be gathered from the inclusion in Indian mythology of the *Apsaras*. Like her counterpart, the Grecian nymph, the *Apsaras* was the mistress of gods and men, and appears frequently in Indian painting and sculpture as a celestial courtesan. Full-breasted and lascivious, she is reputed to have delighted in the temptation of ascetics. So the appearance of the breast in Indian art is further supported by the pronounced sensuality of the *Apsarases*, the heavenly courtesans.

In every direction the roots of the cult of the breast run deep. Vatsyayana was by no means the earliest commentator on sexual techniques. Centuries before Christ, Nandi is reputed to have written a thousand chapters on *Kama*. These were gradually condensed by such authorities as Svetaketu, and Vabhravya, until the ultimate in systematic condensation was finally achieved by Vatsyayana in the *Kāmasūtra*.

But what was the impact of the breast in the context of the daily life of ancient India? How did it appear at home, and in the streets? We have discussed its place and significance in art; but to what extent is art the measure of life? There seems little doubt that the fictions of art are invariably founded upon the facts of life, though suitably extended or modified. This would certainly seem true of the subject in question, for in spite of some disagreement among authorities, there is considerable evidence that from the earliest times to the Muslim conquests, it was customary

49

for Hindu women to wear their breasts exposed, as so often portrayed in the painting and sculpture of the period. Apart from the complete nakedness of the body during erotic activities, Indian women are frequently represented, especially in painting, as they must have appeared in daily life. Here, more passively, they can be seen either naked to the waist, or with the breasts popping, or peeping seductively from their sari-like clothing. Bodices too were often worn, while the adornment of the naked breast with ropes of pearls, and rich, ornate necklaces fashioned from gold and silver and precious stones, would seem to have been as common an occurrence in life as in art.

It is a curious feature, even of the most complex societies, that in spite of social and religious ramifications, the key to their essence is usually contained in solitary symbols—the cross, for instance. Nowhere is this more evident than in the patterns of Indian art, where the female breast is the focus of an entire culture.

Fountain of pleasure—pillow of forgetfulness; her moons rise softly over the yearning face of mankind, offering together the twin joys of *Kama*, and a glimpse, however fleeting, of the shining nirvana.

Yet while India was enjoying her golden and middle ages, Europe was plunged in the darkness of medieval Christendom with its malevolent hatred of sex, and womenkind. On the one hand the breast was a symbol of the good and full life, on the other, a lewd and evil device of the devil to seduce and deprave mankind. For a thousand years the eyes of European painters and sculptors were to be shut tight against its seductions.

3

Exile and Return

She was a plump, well rounded wench, this lass,
Her nose was flat, her blue eyes clear as glass,
Her buttocks broad, her breasts were round and high.
    (The Reeve's Tale.[1] Geoffrey Chaucer, 1340?-1400)

'The Church never succeeded in obtaining universal acceptance of its sexual regulations, but in time it became able to enforce sexual abstinence on a scale sufficient to produce a rich crop of mental disease. It is hardly too much to say that medieval Europe came to resemble a vast insane asylum.'[2]

★

The savage rejection of the body by the medieval Church, its black and bitter hatred of the sexual act, and the insane loathing which it specially reserved for woman, all conspired to strike clean from the face of medieval art any semblance of recognition for the female breast as a symbol of beauty and pleasure.

The milk and honey that flowed from the golden apples of the classic mould were dried at their source under the scorching, sex-hating sun of the medieval sky. The myth of the happy satyr lusting in rumbustious innocence for the panting breasts of nereid or nymph gave place for a thousand years to fantasies of witchcraft and original sin, and the obscene misogyny that placed woman at the centre of all devilry.

[1] Theodore Morrison, *The Portable Chaucer*. (Macmillan, Toronto.)
[2] G. Rattray Taylor, *Sex in History*. (Thames & Hudson.)

Yet in spite of the humiliation and shame to which the flesh was subjected during the dark millennium, there seems little doubt, as Sir Kenneth Clark observes:[1] 'That human beings were still conscious of physical desire, we may assume'; conscious in life at least, although in the art forms of the black ages, the female body was stripped of the last vestige of its natural sensuousness. The breasts withered into small, dry, pitiful protuberances, and until we reach the pot-belly convention of the fifteenth century (Plate 26) there is little of anatomical consequence to distinguish Adam from Eve.

'The whole of medieval art,' writes Sir Kenneth,[1] 'is a proof of how completely Christian dogma had eradicated the image of bodily beauty . . . even in those subjects of iconography in which the nude could properly be represented the medieval artist seems to show no interest in those elements of the female body which we have come to think of as inevitably arousing desire.'

What better example of the rejection of the breast as a sexual feature could one find to illustrate this point, than the appearance of the female figure in the Bamberg Adam and Eve (Plate 28).

The price of original sin was high indeed by this accounting. Woman, the temptress, bereft of all her charms, a pathetic, sterile figure, dry as a stick in the wilderness, and sunk in the black night of eternal guilt and damnation, such was the image the Church sought to project through the artists of the middle ages. Sometimes, as in such figures as the statue from Langham Hall (Plate 27), she is stripped even of her shrivelled protuberances. The ultimate penalty for her sexual guilt has been mercilessly extracted. She is denied even the symbol of her motherhood.

And often, right up to the threshold of the Renaissance, she is hounded in abject shame, hiding her breasts and pudenda with guilty and trembling hands, as in Masaccio's 'Expulsion from Eden'.

Medieval misogyny erupted from deep and seething roots. The official conception of sex as fundamentally sinful, and the consequent abomination of the body, and especially the flesh of woman, emanated from such relentless anti-feminists as Paul of Tarsus, Tertullian of Carthage, and later, St Augustine. (Although in fairness to Paul we must concede that he was certainly the least savage of the trio for he did in fact, however reluctantly, countenance the sexual act between husband and wife.

[1] Sir Kenneth Clark, *The Nude*.

'It is good for a man not to touch a woman. Nevertheless to avoid fornication, let every man have
his own wife, and let every woman have her own
husband.')

The frantic desire of the Church to impose a code of sexual
abstinence upon medieval society sprang from sources more
vicious than Paul's distasteful and morbid misogyny. There is
pure madness in the ravings of Tertullian (c. A.D. 155-222) and
St Augustine (A.D. 354-430). Simone de Beauvoir comments on
these, and upon the nature of the origins of medieval anti-
feminism in *The Second Sex*:

> In her (woman) the Christian finds incarnated the temp-
> tation of the world, the flesh, and the devil. All the
> Fathers of the Church insist on the idea that she led
> Adam into sin. We must quote Tertullian (end of second
> century A.D.): 'Woman! You are the gateway of the devil.
> You persuaded him whom the devil dared not attack
> directly. Because of you the Son of God had to die. You
> should always go dressed in mourning and in rags' . . .
> Christian literature (often) strives to enhance the disgust
> that man can feel for woman. Tertullian defines her as
> 'a temple built over a sewer' . . . St Augustine (A.D.
> 354-430) called attention with horror to the obscene
> commingling of the sexual and excretory organs: '*Inter
> faeces et urinam nascimur.*' Up to the end of the twelfth
> century the theologians, except St Anselm, considered
> that according to the doctrine of St Augustine original
> sin is involved in the very law of generation: 'Con-
> cupiscence is a vice . . . human flesh born through it is
> a sinful flesh,' writes St Augustine. 'The union of the
> sexes transmits original sin to the child, being accom-
> panied since the Fall, by concupiscence.'

The literal acceptance of the story of the Fall, and the blame
attributed to woman for her part in precipitating the first sexual
sin, were the basis of the anti-feminist teachings of the middle
ages. From these beliefs sprang the hostility to sex, and the loathing of the flesh, that drove the warm, seductive body of woman
into a thousand-year exile. Throughout the middle ages her form
was crucified time and again in the images of art. But although

53

the Church sought with increasing desperation, and even madness, to enforce its code of sexual repression,[1] life itself could not be subdued. If the plastic arts stripped the female form of its sensuality, there is a curious and revealing paradox in the quotation from Chaucer which stands at the head of this Chapter.

However strongly the Church may have felt about the need for sexual abstinence, however violently it condemned the pleasures of the flesh, it would be difficult to find a more frank and healthily lustful expression of sensual observation than is contained in these few lines of Chaucer. There is nothing inhibited about this tribute to the joy of a woman's breasts. Throughout his writings the poet clearly reveals that in the late middle ages sexual enjoyment was openly courted by ordinary men and women. In his study, *Sex in History* Rattray Taylor observes that during this period 'Aphrodisiacs were much sought after', that 'Prostitution was extremely widespread', while in matters of attire 'women wore low-necked dresses, so tight round the hips as to reveal their sex, and laced their breasts so high that, as was said, "a candle could be stood upon them". Men wore short coats, revealing their private parts, which were clearly outlined by a glove-like container known as a braguette, compared with which the codpiece was a modest object of attire.'

Evidently the strictures that the Church was able to bring to bear upon the representation of the body in art, it could not, in the last resort, apply to the conduct and behaviour of society.

There is sharp contrast too in the behaviour of medieval priests and nuns. On the one hand we find the most appalling manifestations of sexual repression and, on the other, the flagrantly indulged sexual licence that drew from Villon, consort of dissolute nuns and debauched friars, the lusty stanza which opens his 'Ballade of Ease'—

[1] G. Rattray Taylor writes in *Sex in History*: 'What is less generally realized is the extensive nature of the attempt which was made to limit and control the sexual act *within* the marital relationship. Thus the sexual act must be performed in only one position, and numerous penalties were prescribed for variants, the approach *"more canino"*—which was held to afford the most pleasure—being regarded with especial horror and calling for seven years penance . . . Not content with this, the Church proceeded to cut down the number of days per annum upon which even married couples might legitimately perform the sexual act. First, it was made illegal on Sundays, Wednesdays and Fridays, which effectively removed the equivalent of five months in the year. Then it was made illegal for forty days before Easter and forty days before Christmas, and for three days before attending communion (and there were regulations requiring frequent attendance at communion). It was also forbidden from the time of conception to forty days after parturition. It was, of course, forbidden during any penance.' (Thames & Hudson.)

Athwart a hole in the arras, t'other day,
I saw a fat priest lay on a down bed,
Hard by a fire; and by his side there lay
Dame Sydonic, full comely, white and red:
By night and day a goodly life they led.
I watched them laugh and kiss and play, drink high
Of spiced hypocras; then, putting by
Their clothes, I saw them one another seize,
To take their bodies pleasure. Thence knew I
There is no treasure but to have one's ease.

(From a translation by John Payne)

Although this was written in the first half of the fifteenth century, Villon was still close enough to the spirit of the late middle ages to leave a colourful picture of the robust, bawdy, rollicking way of life that gathered momentum towards the close of the era: a natural and violent reaction to the monstrous repressions of the earlier centuries. This was a fine fanfare for the liberating forces of the Renaissance. There was great sexual licence during the early part of the middle ages, but symptoms of the intense sexual frustration that accompanied the growing censures of the medieval Church are apparent from the many cases of psychoneurotic behaviour that were documented during the later periods. Apart from the countless cases of flagellation, convulsion among nuns,[1] and hysterical pregnancies, Rattray Taylor lists 'the action of Veronica Giuliani, beatified by Pius II, who, in memory of the lamb of God, took a real lamb to bed with her, kissing it and suckling it on her breasts. The desperate frustration of natural instincts is also shown by such incidents as that of St Catherine of Genoa, who often suffered from such internal fires that, to cool herself, she lay upon the ground crying, "Love, love, I can do no more". In doing this she felt a peculiar inclination for her confessor.' Even more astonishing are the incredible excesses of Christine of St Troud (1150-1224) who 'laid herself in a hot oven, fastened herself on a wheel, had herself racked, and hung on the gallows beside a corpse; not content with this, she had herself partly buried in a grave'. Fielding observes: 'She suffered from obsessions which are now generally recognized as transparent sexual hallucinations.'[2]

[1] 'Such hysterical seizures usually bear a close relationship to the unconscious fantasy: in particular, women sometimes exhibit compulsive bodily movements, or become rigid, with the body arched so that the pudenda are thrust forward as in coitus—the so called *arc-en-cercle* position.' (Rattray Taylor, *Sex in History*.)

[2] Rattray Taylor, *Sex in History*.

55

These extraordinary case-histories throw considerable light on the forces of repression that produced, not only a psychopathology of human behaviour, but also of art. The tragic hysteria of these wretched women finds an uncomfortable echo in the morbid shrinking of the breast, and later, in the swollen stomachs that might so easily symbolize the hallucinatory pregnancy, quite apart from any conscious intention on the part of the artist to suggest the immaculate conception.

With the close of the fourteenth century the first crocuses of a new humanism were beginning to appear. Everywhere, although especially in Italy, the black ice of medieval darkness was starting to crack and thaw. The pulse of the rising flood that was to sweep into the Renaissance can be measured already in the humanism of Boccaccio, and the first stirrings of the rediscovery of the culture and civilization of the ancient world. The grime of ten centuries was being scrubbed from the façade of history and the shining humanism of Greek art and philosophy revealed. It was the same humanistic spirit that permeated the work of Chaucer, who himself drew freely upon such classical writers as Ovid for the substance of his plots and tales.

As the European mind slowly disengaged itself from the tyranny of the Church so, little by little, artists began once more to represent the female body with a decreasing sense of fear and shame. Gradually, as the tourniquet of repression was relaxed, she became once again an object of beauty and desire; although the return to her full status as the natural woman was a slow process. The savage sex-hatred of the middle ages died hard.

Tentatively, and with the shy and tender reticence of a young girl revealing her charms for the first time, the breast bares its buds to the clear sunshine of the Renaissance morning. From her exile of a thousand years, woman is now returning into the living light of the artist's warm and loving eye. On the brink of the Renaissance one such typical flowering can be seen in the central figure of the 'Last Judgment'[1] carved in France during the thirteenth century. It is a tender, gently seductive adaptation of the classical model, and would seem to provide the proof that even at this early stage, and in France, artists were able to study, probably fragments, of antique sculpture. Though still Gothic in feeling, this charming, and graceful figure represents the first step in a return journey that would still take three hundred years.

[1] Sir Kenneth Clark, *The Nude*. (John Murray.)

Before the Renaissance finally re-established the sensuous idealism of Greece, the female nude was obliged to grope and pick its
way out of the graveyard of medieval darkness with extreme
caution. Sir Kenneth Clark's remarkable simile of 'Roots and bulbs
pulled into the light'[1] is a graphic and poignant description of the
appearance of the nude figures that populate the scenes of Gothic
painting. 'The bulb-like women and root-like men seem to have
been dragged out of the protective darkness in which the human
body has lain muffled for a thousand years,' he continues. There
is a sense of acute embarrassment about these pale, thin figures,
tugged suddenly into the harsh light of a new convention. (Plate
30). In Rogier van der Weyden's 'Last Judgment', the breast of
the woman struggling in agony and shame over the rockface hangs
like a blob of flesh. There is no sensuality here, only a blind,
inarticulate nakedness. And even when, as in the loving couples
of Bosch (Plate 7), we are confronted with the erotic situation
itself, it is a highly rarefied and relatively sexless atmosphere in
which the lovers caress and unite. In his book *The Millennium*,
Wilhelm Fränger discusses the spirituality of the erotic situation in
Bosch, commenting at one point that here, 'Unbridled sensuality
has calmed down into pure tenderness . . .'[2]

At the close of the middle ages, and in a suitable Gothic form,
Bosch reconciles the eternal battle between sacred and profane
love, in a way that makes acceptable the submission of the body
to those sensual pleasures through which serenity, and union with
God, are ultimately obtained. The central panel of the great triptych, 'The Garden of Earthly Delights', is almost certainly one
of the most extraordinary erotic statements ever committed by an
artist. In spite of the manifest sensuality of the various activities
involved the whole conception is suffused with a spirituality
which makes even the most outrageous conduct seem innocent
and childlike. The women's breasts are quaintly immature and
virginal; hardly even a complement of the delicate sensuality
which the figures and groups pursue with such a quiet and
dignified resignation. No one betrays any overt sign of pleasure.
'The Garden of Earthly Delights' is the ultimate Gothic compromise between the awakening of the 'roots and bulbs' and the
aftermath of the repressions of the medieval era. It is understand-
ably a compromise of caution. But it would be wrong to leave this
astonishing and immensely complex work on a note of mere over-

[1] Sir Kenneth Clark, *The Nude*. (John Murray.)
[2] Wilhelm Fränger, *The Millennium of Hieronymus Bosch*. (Faber & Faber.)

simplification. Wilhelm Fränger's *Millennium* discusses with immaculate scholarship every aspect and implication of the symbolism involved in a masterpiece which establishes perhaps the first real bridge between the rejection of the body and its return, through the humanism of the Renaissance.

Slowly, the warmth returns to the flesh, the breasts blossom, and the belly swells into a huge fertility symbol. The concentration of interest upon the female stomach is another sign of the reacceptance of woman as a legitimate sexual objective, although the approach is oddly oblique. The erotic element is inferred through the appearance of pregnancy. A fact which, presumably, would have made the act of love acceptable since the end product is the asexual ugliness of parturition. This would seem a remarkable psychological explanation of the pot-belly convention in Gothic painting. It would have satisfied both the artist's desire to reaffirm the sexual nature of woman, while appeasing at the same time the moral convention which still associated the sexual act with sin and shame, and demanded some suitable toll as the price of pleasure. The belly proclaims the irrefutable facts of life, but the breasts of the lonely, detached women, are, paradoxically, chaste and virginal (Plate 29).

But the most obvious concession by Gothic artists to the re-emergence of the sexual theme is made in the portraits of Madonnas breast feeding their infants. Hans Baldung's 'Madonna mit den Papageien' (Plate 31) is virginal only in the aspect of the head and features. The child sucks at the nipple with commendable voluptuousness, while the woman's hand caresses and strokes her breast to facilitate the flow of milk. There is more than a hint of incipient sensuality here since the act of breast feeding is in itself an intensely erotic activity fraught, as we now know, with complex Freudian ramifications. The glazed and trancelike ecstasy of the infant, the caressing fingers, and full-blown breast of the mother are deeply erotic. The sensuality of a mother's manipulation of her breast can be felt even more distinctly in the Madonna of the Master of Flémalle, Robert Campin (Plate 32), an earlier example of the oblique eroticism of the Gothic style that delicately foreshadows the lush, pagan voluptuousness of the milk spurting goddess in Rubens' 'War and Peace' (Plate 33).

The mounting tempo of resurgent humanism took many forms. The significance of the individual was recognized, and the right of man to enquire, intellectually and scientifically, into the nature of things, was gradually re-established. The excavation of antique

statues and fragments in Rome[1] exerted a profound influence upon
the artist, leading him to a study of the nude as an object of interest
in its own right. Everywhere the spirit of curiosity was aroused,
and in Germany no less than Italy the body was subjected to
close scrutiny. This is apparent in Dürer's 'Naked Hausfrau'
(Plate 34) and in his 'Women's Bath' (Plate 35). The preoccupation with anatomy that was to become the obsession of Michelangelo, and a lodestar of the Italian Renaissance, is clearly
evident in Dürer's drawings. They were almost certainly taken
direct from the living nude. During the late middle ages, opportunities for the first-hand study of the body could easily have been
obtained by attendance at the public baths. These institutions,
known as *stews*, and often condemned by contemporary moralists,
provided facilities for mixed bathing, and opportunities for casual
sex relations, since many of the baths were also brothels.

Dürer's fascinated observance of the details of the ugly and the
grotesque in his bath scene are a key to the new age. The search
for truth, however distasteful it might sometimes be, was as much
a part of the spirit of the Renaissance as was the quest for an
absolute beauty. The study of nature was a primary interest of
the artists of the period, and here, Dürer spares us nothing. His
inquisitive eye is remorselessly revealing. The remote idealism
of Botticelli for instance (Plate 18), is sharply offset by the disquieting and earthy curiosity of Dürer, and the anatomical dis-
figurements of Signorelli (Plate 36), and Michelangelo (Plate 37)
Here are the opposing faces of the Renaissance Zeitgeist: the
exploration of the realities of nature, and the quest of an arbitrary
absolute. No artist of the Renaissance—and Dürer is essentially a
Renaissance master—exercised a sharper eye for the naturally
grotesque, or the ideally beautiful, than he. His 'Women's Bath'
contrasts the potential ugliness of the breast, the coarse sensuality
of its pendulous form, with its round, firm beauty. This particular
work is in many ways a Renaissance landmark. The subject is
secular, the concentration on anatomical detail marked, and the
whole conception stresses the differences between human beings,
if only here on the plane of physical appearance. To paraphrase
a well-known line, the proper study of mankind is woman. And
yet, in his attempts to picture the real, as opposed to the ideal,
and there is a conflict of these elements in his bath scene, Dürer
cuts sharply across the main objective of Italian Renaissance

[1] Jacob Burckhardt, *The Civilization of the Renaissance in Italy*. Part III. The
Revival of Antiquity.

artists. Clearly this was the desire to re-establish an objective standard of physical beauty, based, not on the harsh facts of reality, but upon the appearance of the pagan goddesses of classical art. The element of classicism in the 'Women's Bath' is curiously offset by the artist's careful documentation of human ugliness. The hideous woman on the right, with her obscene dugs, is a monument to the decay of the flesh, while in contrast, the breasts of the young creature in the centre, firm, and well spaced, are reminiscent of the golden apples of the classic mould. The mortality of the flesh and the immortality of an ideal are subtly intimated in these two renderings of the breast.

The curiosity that led Dürer to his fascinated and self-conscious exploration of the nude presented a problem of real difficulty for European figure draughtsmen, until at last Rembrandt delineated the body with the ease of a master whose knowledge of anatomy was unselfconscious and intrinsic. For Rembrandt drawing was not thought—but breathing. At the outset of the Renaissance, conflict was inevitable. In art, the tug between the resurgence of the classical model, and the relevation of stark reality which the exploring eye of the artist unmasked; the struggle between the sacred and the profane; these were the natural and logical hazards of the new age. The *vita nuova* was fraught with doubts and soul searchings. The scepticism and free thinking of the period produced the mood of divine discontent which ever since has nibbled at the soul of Western man. In Botticelli it created unbearable torment. After painting his pagan allegories, the *Primavera* (*c*. 1748) and the *Birth of Venus* (*c*. 1485), the artist became a fervent supporter of the fanatical reformer, Savonarola, and retreated from poetic and profane subjects into a dark, religious mysticism. He painted little after the execution of his idol in 1498. His wistfully poignant Venus, elegant and refined, arises from the ocean, almost in doubt one feels. Hesitant to reveal her charms, she covers her breasts in the manner of the Venus of Modesty (Medici Venus: Plate 38). And while Botticelli's conception is essentially Renaissance, the spirit of Gothic reticence still prevails, expressing in the master's surpassingly eloquent style the existent conflict of Medieval and Renaissance lines of thought. One might compare Botticelli's Venus with Masaccio's Eve. Although the latter's shame has been transmuted by Botticelli into the less dramatic quality of modesty, the covering of the breasts in each case springs from the common idea that a woman's body is fundamentally an object of disgrace. Eventually of course the problem was resolved in the magnificent frankness of later Italian masters who found in the breast the same, unashamed source of voluptuousness that marks its appearance in classical art. Gradually, the hatred of the body that blackened the middle ages, and spilled over into the early Renaissance, was dispelled. Until the coming of the Reformation, the artist was free from the bondage of religion and the Church and at liberty to pursue the subjects of classical mythology that were to afford the masters of the age their richest opportunities for the portrayal of female beauty.

★

The revival of interest in pagan subjects provided also a rallying point for a general awakening of the spirit of sensualism. The theme of love which the middle ages had treated as a by-product of romance and chivalry, and which Dante's melancholy and languishing mind[1] had elevated to a plane of remote spirituality, was related once more to the tangible pleasures of the flesh. The innate and pervading sensuality of the mythological scene provided the new climate of love. No one has better or more succinctly described the spirit of the rebirth of the golden age than Charles Seltman. Writing of the Renaissance in his book, *Women in Antiquity*, he says:

'The earth was aflame, Love stood at the gate of summer, the satyrs were awake, the dryads had begun their dancing.'

And if we want the living proof that this was indeed the prevailing mood of the time, then let that most civilized inhabitant of Renaissance Italy, Lorenzo de Medici, speak for his age. Patron of the arts, and himself a poet of great ability, he writes in his 'Song for Bacchus'[2]

'How lovely youth is that flies us ever! Let him be glad who will be: there is no certainty in tomorrow.
    This is Bacchus and Ariadne, fair, and each burning for the other: because time flies and deceives, they always stay together in happiness. These nymphs and other

[1] 'My lady is so gentle and modest when she greets others that every tongue trembles and is still, and eyes dare not look upon her. She passes, hearing herself praised, dressed most kindly with humility; and it seems that she is a thing come upon earth from heaven to show forth a miracle . . .' (From *The Penguin Book of Italian Verse*.)
[2] *The Penguin Book of Italian Verse.*

people are always merry. Let him be glad who will be: there is no certainty in tomorrow.

These glad little satyrs are in love with the nymphs, and have laid a hundred ambushes for them in caves and woods: now, heated by Bacchus, they keep up their dancing and their leaping. Let him be glad who will be: there is no certainty in tomorrow.

These nymphs would fain be tricked by them: no one can guard against love but uncouth, ungrateful people: now mingling together, they play instruments and sing always. Let him be glad who will be: there is no certainty in tomorrow.'

Lorenzo makes an eloquent and civilized plea for the life of pleasure, using as his vehicle an allegory of Arcadia. But it is not a shallow or frivolous philosophy. His plea is founded on the belief that love and beauty, and the joys of the senses are a gateway to the realization of 'god'. 'It was thus,' writes Edgar Wind,[1] 'that Lorenzo de Medici observed in *L'altercazione* how his nature contracted whenever he tried to comprehend God through the understanding, but expanded when he approached him through love.'

We are not concerned here with the debauchery and despotism that darkened the Renaissance heaven, but only with the quest of an intensely enlightened age to find again the ideal harmony, and with the desire of the artists and writers of the time to construct a mirror in which would take shape the form of an absolute beauty.

Significantly, this mirror was to be the passions of the gods and goddesses of antiquity. Their form would express the face of the ideal beauty, and if men sought to emulate their passions, or to seek in mortal existence a reflection of their image, as when the lover compares his beloved with a goddess, might they not, even as mortals, aspire to a glimpse of Elysium?

So the perfect form would be the gateway to paradise, and voluptuousness the revelation of divinity.

The ideal, at which Botticelli only hinted, was finally realized, and is perfectly exemplified in the art of Bronzino (Plate 39). Less subtly it appears in Garofalo's 'Amor-Pulchritudo-Voluptas' (Plate 40), and in Lorenzo di Credi's Venus (Plate 41). Before I discuss the nature of the new, and ideal, beauty of the Renaissance,

[1] Edgar Wind, *Pagan Mysteries in the Renaissance*. (Faber & Faber.)

let us consider briefly the acceptance of *voluptas* as the legitimate objective of gods and mortals, since it is only from this ecstasy that the need for an ideal form arises at all.

For man, the abstract is only approachable through the form of the concrete. In the mingling of the flesh with an object of ideal desire, as in the act of love, God, the supreme abstraction, may be revealed to man. Out of the tangible union of lovers springs the ecstasy that discloses the nature of the impalpable divine. The more desirable the object, the more intense the ecstasy. To this end, the erotic art of India is wholly aphrodisiac, offering for the stimulation of the senses, the big-breasted, slim-waisted, broad-hipped image of the Hindu ideal, through whom, in *mithuna*, the *atman* is released into paradise. Similarly, the artists of the Renaissance sought an ideal erotic form as their own point of departure. Mythology and the models of classical art were the raw material from which this ideal was hewn. And alongside the common image of the time, like orchids and cacti springing ludicrously from a bed of daffodils, arose the hermaphrodite and homosexual imagery of Leonardo and Michelangelo. Of these odd men out I will speak later.

The art of the Renaissance is essentially voluptuous. But whereas sensuality in art can uplift and ennoble, in life it will often deprave, especially if it is detached from the ideal. So the voluptuousness of the Renaissance had two faces. The new golden age was also a time of violence and depravity when every crime from incest to murder was indulged with ruthless cynicism by the nobles and the Papacy. So we have on the one hand the negative and corrupting pursuit of pleasure as an end in itself, and on the other, the pursuit of pleasure by men of enlightenment and vision, as a means to an end. It is against the latter objective that the ideal art of the Renaissance must be measured. The sexual freedom of the time transformed the spirit of Dante's humble reverence for woman into a robust acceptance of the body of the beloved as an object of sensual desire, to be embraced and enjoyed on equal terms. Spirituality was held to be an extension of the tangible joys of the flesh. The new, ideal woman was no vaporous image, but one of flesh and blood. In love, it is the identification of the beloved with a physical ideal that raises the pleasures of the senses to the highest peaks of ecstasy and revelation. The true function of ideal art is that it provides an objective against which we can measure the progress of our mortal striving towards the goal of perfection.

63

And since our senses—intellect apart—afford the only loop-holes of escape from the prison of the world, it is natural that the most civilized societies should have pursued these avenues of release, and that the least cultivated and barbaric communities should have rejected them as mere illusion and evil. On the one hand we have the cultures of Greece and India, and on the other the barbarism of the middle ages. The one condition of this argument is of course the necessity to pursue the revelation of the senses, in relation to an ideal. This is what raises the voluptuous-ness of Greek and Renaissance art above the mere lust of the world. Is it not the tragedy of our time that we sink in hollow adoration before the substitute sex symbols of the big-breasted girls who haunt the labyrinths of the popular press? They can inspire only fantasies of sterile lust in the imagination of a sexually immature society. As such they are a poor substitute for the reality of creative sensualism. The erotic images of art are the flowerings of real passion, and spring from the awareness that love can reach beyond the portals of the flesh and the senses, into the lofty halls of paradise itself. The images of debased, erotic photography are the graveyard of our sexual potency, because they have no spiritual extension. They are the ultimate pornography; symptoms of the decline of a civilization; our own.

The question of true *voluptas* is discussed by Edgar Wind in *Pagan Mysteries in the Renaissance*, from which the following quotation is taken:

> 'The use of the same word *voluptas* to designate the most primitive and also the most exalted forms of pleasure was common among Epicureans, and it was recommended by Lorenzo Valla. But in any Neoplatonic argument it would seem like a pointless equivocation since the pleas-ures assigned to heaven and earth would have to be kept strictly apart . . . But it is significant that they were not. Plotinus himself repeatedly advised his disciples to model their expectation of spiritual joy by what they knew of the delusive joys of the senses: "And those to whom the heaven-passion is unknown, may make a guess at it by the passions of earth. Knowing what it is to win what most one loves, let them reflect that here our love is . . . a wooing of shadows that pass and change, be-cause . . . our true beloved is elsewhere, who is ours to enjoy . . . by true possession . . ."

In the joys of mystical exaltation the principle of Pleasure, or man's appetitive impulse, is vindicated against the encroachments of the Stoics, and of the more priggish among the Christian moralists. As Ficino never tired to repeat, the trouble about the pleasures of the senses is not that they are pleasures but that they do not last. It is their transitory, not their enjoyable nature which needs to be amended; and for that purpose the intellect is indispensable. But while the intellect raises us above pleasant delusions, it still detains us below the enjoyment of the real. In reducing the confusion of the senses to reason, the intellect clarifies but it also contracts: for it clarifies by setting limits; and to transcend these limits we require a new and more lasting confusion, which is supplied by the blindness of love. Intellect excludes contradictions, love embraces them.'

Thus we may say that the intellect imposes limits upon our awareness of the infinite by opposing, and seeking to dispel, the contradictory nature of ultimate truth: whereas love, which sees nothing and knows all, precipitates our essence into the bliss of the irrational. For the artists and poets of the Renaissance the springboard was the image of woman: of an ideal woman, infinitely beautiful, and surpassingly sensual. Let us look at this paragon. At a glance her appearance is alarming. The goddess of the new age of gold is not a slender nymph, but a muscular, thick waisted creature, with breasts like beach-balls. Powerfully built, she is the new heavy-weight Venus (Plate 41), the first of a line of voluptuous matriarchs who will succeed her into the canvases of Rubens.

And yet, how superb she is. She commands and dominates every situation, overshadowing the mere presence of man as the sun blots out the last smudge of night. At last, woman, and woman alone, is the centre of all interest, of all beauty, and of all power.[1] The ripe fruits of her breasts, freed of all restraint, assert their glory with exquisite abandon. They provoke, entice, enslave. They speak more eloquently than her enigmatic, classic face, lit by its faint, ambiguous smile. From the extravagant *décolletage* of Bordone's Chloe (Plate 42) they blossom with a

[1] At this point in Western history woman recaptured a position of domination which she has never since relinquished. In fact her authority has increased with the centuries. Today, her dominion, especially in the new matriarchy of America, is virtually absolute.

65

lyrical wantonness. Imploring caresses, they luxuriate in the foreground of Titian's 'Bacchanal' (Plate 43) and, heavy with the milk of paradise, they press into the playful fingers of an infant (Plate 44). How coyly they peep through the Magdalen's tresses (Plate 45), or arrogantly display the magnificence of their form in Veronese's indolent enchantress (Plate 46). The vocabulary of the breast in Renaissance painting is wide, and subtle.

But Venus resurgent follows the pattern of the Hellenistic conception of beauty. Her breasts are those of the goddesses of the last period of Greek art, and more reminiscent of the heavy *mammae* of the Aphrodite of Melos than of the golden apples of Arcadia. The general thickening of the body, and the pronounced emphasis on muscularity, spring partly from a corresponding stress in Hellenistic sculpture, and partly of course (and this may be nearer the true reason) from the fascination of Renaissance artists with the whole question of anatomical study and research. But the problem of the artist's perennial predilection for big breasts still remains. For such is the case.

Why is it that painters and sculptors have usually been loath to minimize the size of the breast, except, for instance, in such special cases as the recognizably hermaphrodite imagery of classical art, or under extreme duress during the medieval period? Perhaps it is because the painter alone can 'see' the breast as pure form in separation from any literary context, or romantic configuration. The more generous this form, the greater its area, the more satisfying as a visual experience. Manet's 'Blonde with Bare Breasts' (Plate 47) would seem to support this view, since the model was not one of the painter's favourite sitters—like Victorine Meurend, the model for Olympia—but a casual subject whose magnificent breasts were sufficient inspiration for the artist. This is essentially a painter's view.

The poet on the other hand is more willing to concede a reduction in size, and indeed, it is from the writer rather than the artist that the idea of small breasts, as an ideal, emanates. Greek writers were constantly comparing them with apples. In a fragment of writing Crates not only compares them with apples, but even likens them to the fruits of the strawberry tree.[1]

That small breasts were also the passion of some Renaissance poets, one gathers from Tasso (1544-95) who voices the apple ideal in his *O bella età de l'oro*:

[1] Crates (CAF., I. 142) (Hans Licht, *Sexual Life in Ancient Greece*.) (Routledge & Kegan Paul.)

Then Cupids, without bows or torches, carolled softly among
flowers and plants; shepherds and nymphs sat mixing caresses
and whispers with their words, and kisses with their whispers,
tightly clinging; the young virgin displayed her fresh roses
nakedly which she now keeps hidden by a veil, and the small,
unsweetened apples of her breasts; and often was the lover seen
to play with the beloved in river or in lake.
(The Penguin Book of Italian Verse)

One of the few Renaissance painters who complement this
conception in pictorial form is Piero di Cosimo (Plate 48). But
the intense individuality of his vision sets him apart from the
prevailing manner of his age. Although his subject matter is
essentially that of the Renaissance, the tiny, apple-like breasts
darting from the thick trunks of his women are almost certainly
a personal foible and in no sense an expression of the aesthetic
vision of the age.

In whatever way she evolves from the classical model, the standard Venus of the Renaissance is essentially a heavy-weight,
armed with the bulky breasts of the Hellenist tradition.

Why are painters and sculptors less willing of their own accord
to depict the breast in small, rather than large forms? The answer
I think must be sought in psychology rather than aesthetics.

From the moment of birth, more or less, the breast dominates
the whole field of experience during the first few months of our
existence. It is the mountain from whose rushing springs we draw
the very substance of our being. It is our point of departure into
sleep. You do not have to be much of a psychologist to infer from
this the significance of our preference for any depiction which
represents the breast as a full, fat form. The apple breast conception may satisfy certain aesthetic susceptibilities but, this
apart, it can only symbolize the aridness of virginity. Inevitably,
it is the psychological, rather than the aesthetic requirements of
our being, that dominate and control. One has only to consider
the Venus of Willendorf (Plate 49) to appreciate this fact. It is
significant enough that one of the earliest pieces of sculpture in
existence should be a fertility symbol. Evidently our remote
ancestors were as breast conscious as the film magnates of the
twentieth century.

To the painter and the sculptor the physical forms of life are,
in themselves, pre-eminently important. But the poet 'sees'
figuratively, rather than literally, so that one would naturally

expect the ideal of small breasts to emanate from him. When Tasso writes of the 'unsweetened apples' of the breast his vision is essentially figurative. An artist could not paint 'unsweetened apples'; only physically small breasts. And even though he was inspired by Tasso's figurative vision, he would not as a matter of course convey this idea to the spectator. It is in the art of love that the figurative vision of the poet comes into its own, for women are won by figurative comparisons—'your breasts are like pears, and your mouth like crushed roses'—even though they are literally seduced.

The classicism of Leonardo presents an intriguing and special problem. By all accounts his interest in mythology was slight. Yet his depictions of men and women, are almost always hermaphrodite in essence. In this sense he would appear, at least superficially, to support an aspect of the classic revival since the blending of male and female characteristics in the aesthetic image was of course a feature of classic sculpture. But the re-creation of this quality by Leonardo, apparent in a conception of Leda which we know only from copies (Plate 50), sprang not from any conscious desire to emulate this facet of the spirit of classicism, but from the simple fact that the artist was himself a homosexual —a homosexual, moreover, of immense sensitivity, and a metaphysician of genius, who sought to forge a supra-erotic image that would blend the polarities of male and female. Why should not Brahma have looked like this before he split himself into the many through desire?[1] Is it conceivable that Leonardo could have known something of Hindu philosophy? Or that he could somehow have seen something of Indian art?

Sir Kenneth Clark refers to the 'oriental prominence'[2] of the breasts of Leda. Yet the chances would seem all against the likelihood that Leonardo had studied Hindu philosophy, or had seen anything of Indian art. Nevertheless he has conceived here—as elsewhere in his art—a composite sexual image, in which male characteristics predominate. Curiously, this is perfectly in accord with the Hindu idea of the male god containing within himself the *sakti*, or female principle, which can be projected, and detached, from the body of the male.

Has Leonardo approached in this extraordinary conception the oneness of Brahma, the supreme male force? The conception of

[1] The subject of the picture is incidental to the conception of Leda who is quite isolated from her setting.
[2] Sir Kenneth Clark, *The Nude*. (John Murray.)

68

the ultimate divinity as essentially male would also meet the requirements of Leonardo's homosexuality. And if, in this vision of Leda, he has opened the shutters of the mind upon a vision of paradise in which all conflict is resolved, then his composite sexual image has far wider implications than the hermaphroditism of classic art which sprang solely from the sexual dilemma of the times. So cosmic is the art of Leonardo, that while he neatly fulfils the objective requirements of anatomical fashion, and to some extent, those of mythology, he transcends these cloying limits as does no other artist of the Renaissance. His mysticism is perhaps the most exalted in the history of Western art.

Michelangelo his great contemporary is shipwrecked on the reefs of anatomical study. Leonardo skims their dangers with immense skill.

Whatever else she may symbolize, Leda is obviously an allegory of the miracle of generation. And yet, one senses the reluctance of the artist to concede the intrusion of the female into an essentially male kingdom. Only grudgingly does he confer the breasts and the characteristic female swing of the hip upon a figure which is otherwise that of an elegant, muscular male. The cold, remote smile, so characteristic of Leonardo, suggests the artist's aloofness from the world, and his possession of a divine secret. In fact his Leda is not a naked woman at all, but the receptacle for a dream. She is clothed in a finely spun veil of pure thought that removes her from the corroding touches of the world. Her breasts are not bare in the sense that Chloe's are naked in Bordone's sylvan image (Plate 42). Nor, in spite of any comparison one might reasonably draw between their 'oriental prominence' and the erotic qualities of the breast in Indian art, are they sexual features. Leda's plump globes are passionless and tranquil. She is the ocean beyond desire into which has flowed and mingled all the rivers of human lust. Here there is only peace. She is the point at which the act of love transcends the carnal and is lost in the infinite. She is ecstasy. She is bliss. But she is not desire. Thus Leonardo's mysticism provokes thought. All his imagery is clothed in a gossamer mantle of exalted apperception. His personalities, places and situations are the crystalline residue of his intellectual and mystical refining. For us, his imagery is the living form of his marvellous thought; for him, it was, perhaps, the nest after the bird had departed into unchartable flight.

The rapt transcendence of Leonardo's vision removed his art far from the vale of the world. He soars above the Renaissance.

Anatomy did not shackle him as it did Michelangelo. To the existence of women he was merely indifferent, whereas in Michelangelo we can sense an active hostility to the female. He considered a woman's body grossly inferior to that of a man's, and many of his studies for subjects involving the female figure were drawn from male models. There seems little doubt that Michelangelo's affliction was both more limiting and more psychopathic than Leonardo's. It was the source of torment and personal melancholy.

In his portrayal of the female breast Michelangelo gives vent to his hatred of the opposite sex. His sculpture of 'Night' (Plate 52) for the Medici Chapel in Florence is brutal and contemptuous. I am not concerned here with the greatness of the sculptor's overall conception—'Night' is only one of the figures he provided for the Medici Chapel—but solely with the light this particular figure throws upon his attitude to woman. For a draughtsman of such immense genius, how does one excuse the loathsome deformation of the breasts which the artist has perpetrated in this monstrous image Only I think if one accepts their ill-drawn ugliness as the sculptor's protest against what he considered the hideousness of the female form. Where Leonardo's perversion opened for him a magic casement, it rooted Michelangelo in his black obsession with the writhing muscles of the young men who dominated his erotic fantasies. It held him earthbound and turned to gall his reaction to the essential softness of the forms of a woman's figure. Leonardo made his peace with the female breast by a mystical transmutation; Michelangelo resented, and resisted, its very existence. For him the breasts of a woman were shapeless lumps, like the dugs of a cow; a gross slander upon the divine form of the male torso. He was quite unable to accept the tender voluptuousness of a woman's breasts, or even to compromise between this quality and his concern with anatomy, as did the lesser masters of the Renaissance. Michelangelo rejected the body of woman as savagely as any medieval misogynist. Not on theological grounds of course, but because his homosexuality was remorselessly and pathologically anti-feminist. Unlike many homosexuals, he would have no truck with women, and certainly not aesthetically. No authority I am sure would seek to construe the artist's friendship with Vittoria Colonna as anything but a companionship of the intellect. His drawings of Vittoria are hard and passionless. If his soul yearned to rise above the constrictions of his affliction—as did that of Leonardo—it must surely have failed since so many of his creations depict the anguish of figures

70

struggling to free themselves from the chains of some intolerable bondage But though his spirit cried out, in this respect at least he remained earthbound.

The new classicism, an ideal which embraced the concept of 'regular beauty', found little expression in the asexualism of Leonardo, or the misogyny of Michelangelo. The sensuous paganism of the age was essentially the province of painters who could enter wholeheartedly into the arcadian spirit of antiquity, neither questioning the subjects of mythology as did Botticelli, nor esotericizing them as did Leonardo. The new age of gold is best mirrored in such smoothly flowing painters as Bronzino, Correggio (Plate 51) and of course, Titian (Plate 56). Here we may see displayed, for its own sake, the form of the new ideal. In the art of these masters the goddess of love reigns supreme. The basis of her calm, serene beauty is symmetry. Her features are carved with absolute regularity, her breasts are twin globes perfectly matched. She is the prototype of that ideal of regular beauty that was to exert such a disastrous influence upon the pseudo-classicism of the nineteenth century.

One must remember that although the classicism of the Renaissance was already secondhand, it succeeded where every other neo-classical movement has since failed, for the simple reason that whereas the Renaissance rediscovery of antique art was a literal uncovering of the past, later attempts to emulate this precedent were based upon a series of carefully combined excuses. The excuse for David's neo-classicism was the idea of discipline and order. The excuse for the neo-classicism of the late nineteenth century was the desire to express sexual themes in a safe and 'respectable' form.

At the close of the sixteenth century, the concept of an ideal, regular beauty was already beginning to pall. The heavy symmetry of Titian's goddesses marked the sunset of the classic dream. Though we may seek perfection, its acquisition, even in art, is ultimately unbearable. It stifles. We cannot breathe in its oppressive embrace and yearn for a more human image, complete with all those familiar blemishes that mark the human condition. The red-gold and russet-bronze of Titian mark the end of a convention. The age of the ideal woman, muscular, big-breasted, and impeccably regular, would soon melt into the fluid, baroque style of Rubens, with his passion for real, human plumpness, and his general disregard for the rules of the classic convention.

For almost the first time since Dürer described with taut,

71

THE MOONS OF PARADISE

inquisitive eye, the naked body of his Nuremberg *Hausfrau,* Rubens extricates the female figure from the chains of a stifling convention. And while he still makes full use of allegorical and mythological situations as a setting for his new conception of woman, he shapes at last a creature of flesh and blood, who can sing the praises of the bountiful blessings of nature. His goddesses are of the earth and, as women, they herald the realism of Rembrandt.

Apart from the search for an ideal standard of physical beauty—one that would match *L'amor divino* men dreamed of in the cell of their mortal coil—the feature of the time which had most bearing upon the appearance of the female breast in art and fashion was the relative freedom of Renaissance society from any sense of sexual guilt.[1]

Sex was accepted as an intrinsic element in the life of the whole man. Sexual relations were freely pursued and indulged. Adultery was rife. 'All passion,' writes Burckhardt, 'was directed to the married woman.' In Part IV of *The Civilization of the Renaissance in Italy* he continues:

> 'Under these circumstances it is remarkable that, so far as we know, there was no diminution in the number of marriages . . . Nor did the race sink, either physically or mentally, on this account . . .'

Sex was an activity to be enjoyed, either as a pleasure in its own right or as the point at which the dream of ideal love could meet and mingle with the divine.[2] Either way, the savage inhibitions of the middle ages were swept away.

Once again, as in the classical periods of Greek and Indian civilization, the courtesan enjoys a position of respect and influence. She is an honoured and much valued member of her

[1] Rattray Taylor writes in his *Sex in History:* 'The sense of guilt in sexual matters having faded, men no longer required to employ psychic energy in repressing their desires and such energy was therefore available for the creation of works of art. As Freud has argued, for the intellectual engaged in purely cerebral labours, sexual abstinence may be advantageous; for the creative artist it is always disastrous.'

[2] Burckhardt writes in *The Civilization of the Renaissance* (Allen & Unwin): 'When we come to look more closely at the ethics of love at the time of the Renaissance, we are struck by a remarkable contrast. The novelists and comic poets give us to understand that love consists only in sensual enjoyment, and that to win this, all means, tragic or comic, are not only permitted, but are interesting in proportion to their audacity and unscrupulousness. But if we turn to the best of the lyric poets and writers of dialogues, we find in them a deep and spiritual passion of the noblest kind, whose last and highest expression is a revival of the ancient belief in an original unity of souls in the Divine Being.'

72

society. Like the *hetairae* of Greece and the courtesans of Vatsy-ayana's day, she is the friend and mistress of men of quality and distinction. Statesmen, artists and poets all worship at her shrine. From the seclusion of her home she subtly exerts her influence, holding court like a queen.

I remarked earlier on the fact that periods of great cultural achievement have always accorded an honoured place to the courtesan. Her free-standing figure completes, without obligating, the need of the creative personality for sexual and intellectual refreshment. Marriage imposes obligations in return for such favours. In the wasteland of the middle ages—as today in the sexually sterile setting of the Western world—there was no courtesan class, only the common prostitute. As such, woman is simply an instrument for the alleviation of a momentary lust. She cannot be compared with her cultivated cousin, the intelligent, educated and elegant courtesan of Greece, India or Renaissance Italy.

Something of the sophistication and elegance with which she was accredited during the Renaissance is clear from Bartolommeo Veneto's 'Portrait of a Courtesan' (Plate 53). The hair has been stiffened with gum and gilded. The jewellery is exquisitely taste-ful, while the garland and the flowers add a pastoral note to the studied sophistication of the conception. The naked breast is small and youthful, in striking contrast to the fact that the woman is relatively mature: certainly in her early thirties one would imagine, to judge from the worldliness of the eyes, the calculating set of the mouth, and the first, tender bulge of a double chin. One wonders if the painter may have intentionally idealized the breasts along the lines of the golden apples of the classical conception? There is no sense here of the heavy-weight convention that marked the character of Renaissance figure painting. The breasts of Veneto's conception are closer to the figurative notion of Tasso's 'unsweetened apples'.

And since the painter was a Venetian, the style of attire may well depict an exquisite fashion of the time. This was the cele-brated *espoitrinement à la façon de Venise* in which rouge was applied to the exposed breasts and nipples.

How alarming by contrast is the prostitute image of our own time. Exposed to the incessant ravages of the most fleeting and tawdry lusts, the body degenerates into a shapeless pulp. Rouault's 'Prostitutes' (Plate 54) present the tragic reverse of a noble profession. They stand in the apathy of decay, a moving contrast

73

with Bartolommeo Veneto's polished and leisurely courtesan.

Though there is perhaps more general—and practical—knowledge of sex matters among young people today than ever before, and while adultery is common, and divorce almost a fashion, sex in the Christian world is still associated with those fantasies of sin and guilt that drove the middle ages to the brink of madness. Inevitably in such a setting the prostitute is a symbol of shame and degradation.

The Renaissance search for an ideal form permeated the whole structure of its aesthetic, social, and moral life. We have seen, briefly, how this ideal took shape in the painting and poetry of the age. But perfection is a hard master. It demands our undivided and constant attention. As its servant, we can never relax. To seek it in life must inevitably lead to bitter disappointment. To achieve it in art must pave the way for the sterilities of mannerism that inevitably succeed the first generation of innovators. The classic revival of the Renaissance died quite naturally, and of old age, in the canvases of Titian. Thereafter, the body of woman, restored at last to its rightful place at the centre of man's world, was free to live and breathe as flesh and blood. When Rubens cut the corsets of the classic dream he released a real woman. The age of the goddess, peerless and remote, was over. Rubens' portrait of his second wife, Hélène Fourment (Plate 55) is the moment of release; a turning point in the history of the artist's conception of woman. From this warm and living reality there would be no turning back. Henceforth the painter will mark her faults with a loving hand, and the lover will melt in tenderness before the sweet irregularity of the beloved's breasts.

Now, safely returned from exile, woman will continue her journey through the mirrors of art. She will be loved and martyred, adored and humiliated, upon the anvil of man's passions. And her joy and her suffering will be reflected in the flesh of the painter's *matière*, and the bones of the sculptor's stone . . .

4

The Map of Love

Show me thy feet, show me thy legs, thy thighs,
Show me those fleshy principalities;
Show me that hill where smiling love doth sit,
Having a living fountain under it . . .
(To Dianeme: Robert Herrick)

When Rubens and Rembrandt set free the body of the beloved
they liberated simultaneously the eye of the artist. Since the
seventeenth century painters and sculptors have been free to
contemplate the landscape of a woman's form with a truly naked
eye. Undimmed by the cataract of inhibiting conventions, they
have gazed with clear, bright, loving, and intimately exploring
eyes at the hills and valleys of this other Eden. They have seen
the world of a woman's body for what it is. Beyond the psychoneurotic imagery of medieval art, or the lush myth of Renaissance
idealism, they have portrayed the ecstasy and the sadness of the
woman of flesh and blood.

What Herrick dreamed in the glade of his poet's eye, they have
revealed on canvas, and in stone. And beyond his gay and frivolous
sensualism they have seen the tender, the sad, even the brutal
and satiric. Let us see . . .

The fleshy principalities of Renoir (Plate 57) are the most
loving and relaxed delineations of the female breast in the history
of Western art. His women are the loved ones; serene and secure
in the knowledge that every movement, every curve, every line of
their body is the centre of a man's constant adoration. One can
sense in the exquisite unselfconsciousness of their actions the
unconcern with which a woman in the prime of love will abandon

75

the sight of her body to the gaze of her lover, happy in the knowledge that he will find in the contemplation of her relaxed nakedness the unexpected source of sensual refreshment. The sudden revelation of an unfamiliar beauty of line, or shape, or form, as she dries her body, or combs her hair, will strike him to the quick of his soul. When a woman is loved, and while her body has the power to arouse desire in the bones of her lover, she will have no hesitation in permitting him to scrutinize the most intimate details of her personal *toilette*. He may enjoy the spectacle of her struggle, as with dangling breasts she endeavours to fasten her brassière, or survey at his leisure their tender droop as she bends forward to trim her toenails. She will take pride in the fact that she can safely abandon herself to his adoring sight.

It is this sense of the absolute giving of the sight of her body to the eye of the beloved, without reserve, or stint, or anxiety, that permeates Renoir's nudes. They are the loved ones and, as Simone de Beauvoir writes in her study of woman—*The Second Sex* (Jonathan Cape)—

'Love is the developer that brings out in clear, positive detail the dim negative, otherwise as useless as a blank exposure. Through love, woman's face, the curves of her body, her childhood memories, her tears, her gowns, her accustomed ways, her universe, everything she is, all that belongs to her, escape contingency and become essential: she is a wondrous offering at the foot of the altar of her god.'

Here, everything is essential, nothing is merely contingent. There is no tension in the brimming, yet utterly relaxed, 'principalities' of Renoir's women. It is the high summertime of love, the heyday of ecstasy and delight, when the breast in abandon relaxes from the tensions of passion, and woman, released temporarily from the bondage of loving, can set about the business of restoring her tumbled hair, and bathing away the salt of love's exertions.

But the rhythms of life alternate between tension and relaxation. The muscles of the body contract and extend; harden and grow soft. When a woman lifts her arms above her head, her breasts, raised like a portcullis over the plateau of the thorax and the rolling hill of the stomach, are charged with dynamic tension. At such times the breasts, aggressive and thrusting, reveal the incomparable beauty of their curves, running like arcs of fire against the tall sky. At such moments the silhouette of the breast transcends the merely sensual to integrate with the cosmic patterns of nature. Earth and sky and the forms of the body are fused in a tense, dramatic unison, as here, in Reg Butler's figure of a woman (Plate 58). The suggestion is even more intensely conveyed by Henry Moore's figure of a pregnant woman rising in her mountainous parturience from the roots of nature (Plate 59).

The dynamic opposition of volume and space is one of the most dramatic aspects of nature. In the charged forms of the young Yugoslav sculptress Olga Jancic, the same tension is played out in the form of a drama. In her 'Lovers' (Plate 60), the sexes, tensed for battle, face each other like warriors armed to the teeth, ready to spring, and strike. In such moments, a woman's breasts, poised like protective shields, face the horned god, the demon of her dreams, the maker and the slayer of her body. For a moment only the tension of her breasts will express the illusion of her independence. But soon she will lay aside the shields and, in the act of surrender, yield the rivers of her flesh to the consuming embrace. Then she will melt, and mingle, trading her beauty, her desire, the surrender of her very soul for the bliss of identification with the loved one. The moment of union is expressed by Rodin with surpassing poignancy in *Le Baiser* (Plate 61). The breasts are streams now, flowing beyond time and place into the shoreless sea, where all the pangs of self are neutralized at last, in the heart of the running tides. The desire for identification with the beloved is the core of the lover's striving. Somewhere in Garcia Lorca a woman says of her lover: 'When I look into his eyes I feel I can taste his blood.' She might have continued—'O love, who demands all that there is of me; you, who would enter into the structure of my bones, and sit in the temple of my eyes: who would mark my pulse with the tempo of your blood, and devour my entrails in the black annihilation of a kiss . . .' All this the lovers know, as they blend. The trembling humility, the fearful yet ecstatic joy of the surrender of self: the whole miraculous literature of love is read out in the woman's utter giving of herself, and the man's inexpressibly tender touch as he lays the dove of his hand upon her thigh. *Le Baiser* is the only great work by a Western artist that approximates in spirit to the *mithuna* couples of Indian art. And it far exceeds anything I know as an expression of man's overwhelming tenderness for woman.

To surrender, is to relax. In the patterns of love, as in sleep, the body renounces its tensions. The breasts fall apart, spreading

77

wide their ivory hills. The map changes, hills and valleys shift, and in their movement reveal new prospects for the eye. The alignments of desire as each movement of the body shuffles and reorientates its elements were noted no less keenly by the eye of Baudelaire than by that of Boucher. The poet's vision of this ecstasy conjures a picture that is close to the sumptuous eroticism of Boucher and Fragonard, two masters of the portrayal of the sensual relaxations of the female body.

In *Les Bijoux* the poet writes of the delight and ravishment of his eye by the insinuating subtleties of the body as it moves upon the couch. He notes too the characteristic paradox of the innocence and wantonness which women, either by design, or instinct, so skilfully combine in the appearance of their nakedness.

> '*She was lying down and let herself be loved, and from the divan's height she smiled for pleasure at my passion, deep and gentle as the sea, rising towards her as towards its cliff.*
>
> *Her eyes fixed on me, like a tame tiger, with a vague dreamy air she tried various positions, and ingenuousness joined to lubricity gave a new charm to her metamorphoses;*
>
> *And her arm and her leg and her thigh and her loins, polished as oil, sinuous as a swan, passed before my calm, clear-sighted eyes; and her belly and breasts, those clusters of my vine . . .*'
>
> (*The Penguin Book of French Verse*)

The imagery might so easily describe the seductiveness of Boucher's Venus as she surrenders to the caresses of Mars (Plate 62).

Rex Whistler in one of his illustrations for A. E. W. Mason's *Königsmark* has also expressed with great charm the falling apart of the ivory hills in the moment when a woman's body relinquishes every tension, and the belly and breasts become the clusters of the vine, aching to be gathered (Plate 63). In the playful scenes of Fragonard, the map of love is portrayed with a rapturous lightness. The breasts become airy as the puffed clouds in a summer sky, and if his maidens are sometimes remote from the reality of life, they possess enough of the essential quality of youth to make them infinitely more feasible than the cold beauties of Renaissance art (Plate 66). When Herrick wrote 'Upon the Nipples of Julia's Breast', or dreamed of his sweet Dianeme, he could hardly have imagined a more likely crystallization of his

78

vision than the maidens of Fragonard and Boucher (Plate 64).

> Have ye beheld with much delight
> A red rose peeping through a white?
> Or else a cherry double graced
> Within a lily's centre placed?
> Or ever marked the pretty beam,
> A strawberry shows half drowned in cream?
> Or seen rich rubies blushing through
> A pure smooth pearl, and orient too?
> So like to this, nay all the rest,
> Is each sweet niplet of her breast.

('Upon the Nipples of Julia's Breast'.
Robert Herrick)

In *The History of Underclothes*,[1] the authors claim that in the eighteenth century 'the centre of erotic attraction had, in fact, changed'. They go on to say that 'During the seventeenth century it had been the breasts, either completely exposed, or very nearly so. One notes for instance that all through the patterns of Restoration drama the breasts are specially admired and freely spoken of, and that the women characters accept such compliments with approval.'

This is quite consistent with Herrick's passion for the breast, with many of Lely's portraits, and with the daring *décolletage* of Stuart fashion. But where painting and the graphic arts are concerned, you could hardly find an age which pays greater homage to the luxury of the breast than do the French painters of the eighteenth century, or one which exploits its appearance with more malicious effect than do the English caricaturists of the period. The eighteenth century is still the age of the breast. And curiously, the century that on the one hand conceived the breast solely as an erotic feature, saw it also as a mirror in which to satirize the social and psychological character of a nation. This remarkable contrast throws considerable light upon the respective character of British and French society. For instance, Clodion's seraphic vision of Psyche borne heavenwards by the sheer buoyancy of her breasts (Plate 65) sprang directly from the erotic requirements of a small ruling hierarchy, the French court. The map of love was displayed as a stimulant for the refined tastes of a powerful minority whose blasé sensibilities needed the boost of the effervescent rococo style. Even so it might be argued that the

[1] C. Willett and Phillis Cunnington. *The History of Underclothes*. (M. Joseph.)

most exquisite and transcendent manifestations of the erotic spirit are those which rise from the couch of luxury. Yet the increase in wealth and political power which arose in England during the mid-eighteenth century produced nothing that corresponded with the superbly refined eroticism of French decorative and rococo art. Characteristically, the limitation has a psychological rather than an economic basis. At this time British painters were relatively unskilled in the art of figure painting, and yet, this deficiency apart, it can be argued that the English, with a few notable exceptions[1] have no heritage of sensual refinement. The lusty references in Restoration drama are largely a foretaste of the coarse and bawdy treatment of the breast in eighteenth-century caricature.

In late eighteenth-century England the rise of aesthetic elegance is confined to the design of houses and furniture. The fact is I think sufficiently expressive of the Englishman's instinctive desire to display the extent of his wealth and power in such safe manifestations of affluence as the great house and its accoutrements. And while the fine ladies of the eighteenth century do of course appear in the portrait painting of the time, they do so as symbols of respectability, rather than of luxury and sensuality. They are safe, solid, and grey—a fact which is of course quite consistent with the Englishman's natural sense of the hypocritical in all matters relating to sex. The underlying vulgarity and savagery of his attitude to women is invariably masked by the pretence of 'respectability and decency', a pose which he feels it necessary to project in visual terms. What else is the bowler hat but a symbol of this hypocrisy?

Consequently, the poor Englishwoman has come to believe that the true function of her destiny as a woman is to behave 'respectably and decently'. No matter how deeply and passionately she may secretly yearn for the ardours of real love, she wastes in bitter and arid frustration while her menfolk indulge their puny sexuality in the dirty story, and the prostitute's embrace.

The Englishman expresses his resentment of women, and his embarrassment in their presence, by adopting the crude and boisterous airs of the adolescent schoolboy. For him, the map of love is not an exquisite pattern of sensual features, but an excuse for brutish fun poking. A woman's breasts become 'tits', mere lumps of flesh to be sniggered about. Her buttocks, the luxurious

[1] Elizabethan love poetry would qualify for exception, and so would a notable eccentric like Herrick.

forms that so enthralled the sensuous eye of Rubens, Fragonard, and Boucher, are graded down to the schoolboy's 'bum', a subject fit only for the raucous nomenclature of the fifth form. 'The Bum Shop' by Thomas Rowlandson (Plate 67) is a robust comment on the fashion for false 'bums', 'rumps', or 'culs postiches' that appeared during the last quarter of the eighteenth century. It is also a maliciously revealing comment on the backside obsession of the time. The spirit is pure schoolboy. Newton's 'Nymphs Bathing' (Plate 68), a devastating parody on the current fashion for engraving copies of similar subjects by third-rate Italian painters such as Cipriani, contains all the elements of the immature response to the female figure which is so characteristically English —A woman is 'all tits and bottom'. With the exception of her place in Hogarth's moral situations, the whole range of eighteenth-century English caricature treats the subject of a woman's figure with a coarse eye and a vulgar mind. Rowlandson reflects the mood of the period with brilliant malice. He is a far more important and revealing witness of his time than Hogarth. As an observer, purely and simply, he stands on the touchline of his age, and is not involved in the game. Unlike Hogarth he did not need to contrive the forms of his art for the sake of the axe he wished to grind. The topography of Hogarth's localities ring true enough, but his people, and the situations in which they are set, are mainly symbolic. He is anxious to say something 'big'; to convey a moral message. Rowlandson on the other hand has nothing of moral importance to say, only facts to record; only modes, and fashions, and appearances to state. His exaggerations are purely an intensification of real situations; a common enough practice among caricaturists at any time.

In 'A Drunken Officer with Two Ladies of the Town' (Plate 69) and 'The Landing at Greenwich' (Plate 70), Rowlandson presents a picture of a brash, vulgar age, completely lacking in sexual finesse. Generalizations may be dangerous, but in the end, they are the only way in which we can recreate a picture of the character of societies. History is a method of evaluating facts within a framework of generalization.

In the light of this contention, and in face of the evidence of art and literature, there seems little doubt that England during the second half of the eighteenth century was a curious mixture of elegance and vulgarity, with a distinct coarseness in everything pertaining to matters of sex. Rowlandson's sowish women and roistering tarts, sporting their breasts like so much meat, express the basic coarseness of the age. Here, desire is mere animal heat, and the fleshy principalities a vulgar joke.

It is men who shape the destiny of women. An age which exalts their sex as did the poets and artists of the Renaissance will produce women of rare beauty and exalted sensuality, for women are fired by the dreams of men and will strive to match them. The fastidious and subtle sensuality of the rakes of the French court shaped the exquisite voluptuousness that found expression even in the fashions of the day (Plate 72). And so, the sexual vulgarity of the English male produced a race of trollops. This is not to suggest that women of voluptuousness were unknown in France before the eighteenth century, or women of coarseness in England before the age of Rowlandson. But I think it is reasonable to argue that when the character of a society has crystallized, has hardened into its final form, it will find its most perfect and revealing reflection in the mirror of its arts. Like the hand that regulates the flame of a lamp, the artist adjusts his vision of an age, so that in his art we can study its character, and quality, in the clearest light. This is certainly the main function of caricature. For the Englishman of the late eighteenth century, as Rowlandson so often shows, a woman's body was little more than a pigsty in which to rummage for sexual scraps. And even the pathos of age is the subject of brutal ridicule. The breasts in their decrepitude are objects of fun (Plate 71). One has only to compare this savage conception of age with Rodin's deeply moving portrayal of a similar subject (Plate 73) to appreciate the essential difference between the French and English approach to the problem of interpreting the meaning of a woman's body. The one is sympathetic, the other brutal. Yet at any point in its history, in old age no less than in youth, a woman's body retains its power to evoke emotion; certainly feelings of tenderness. One can hardly contemplate the overwhelming pathos of Rodin's bronze without being stirred in the roots of one's soul. Reflecting on the dry leaves of the old woman's breasts a man who has loved women with tenderness might even yet imagine the love they could have known, and inspired, in that long ago summer when they hung in all their ripeness, like the clusters of the vine . . .

Perhaps the most intriguing problem that arises from the study of the female figure as it appears in the mirrors of art is the mystery of the exposure of the breasts. I say 'mystery', since although we possess conclusive evidence that both Minoan and Renaissance fashions made allowance on occasions for the complete exposure of the breasts and nipples, there still remains considerable doubt among costume authorities as to whether, the Venetians apart, European women ever did in fact wear their bosoms completely exposed. And by complete exposure I mean not simply *décolletage*, however daring, but the clear exposure of the nipples.

The problem is of great interest since there are so many depictions, particularly by French and English artists of the late eighteenth century, that would seem to point to the existence of such a fashion. There are two main sources of pictorial evidence: English caricature, and contemporary French fashion plates. English caricaturists, notably Rowlandson, frequently depict prostitutes and women of the lower classes with their breasts freely exposed. To what extent such nakedness was ever a fact is a matter for argument. The low cutting of the stays, the pushing upward of the breasts by wadding and whalebone, and the general looseness of the surrounding garments would certainly have forced the nipples pretty close to the point of exposure, but it may well be that in the main this final touch was only given by the artist? There is more solid evidence however that in France the fashion was an actual fact, and not simply a figment of the artist's imagination. Recently, I discussed the subject with Mr James Laver. He was most helpful: 'From around 1780 to 1810 the chances of seeing an exposed nipple in French high society were pretty good!' It is an authoritative observation, well supported by a great many contemporary fashion plates in which the nipples are quite bare. There is nothing comparable in English fashion apart from some theatrical costume and, much earlier, some of Inigo Jones' designs for masque costumes which allow for the complete exposure of the breasts (Plate 74). But in the eighteenth century, apart from an entertaining incident involving Elizabeth Chudleigh, Countess of Bristol, and self-styled Duchess of Kingston,[1] there is nothing which suggests that the nipples were bared on occasion, as in French costume. Such plates as one finds in a *Gallerie des Modes* and *Costumes Français* are in the nature of pure documentation and would appear therefore to throw conclusive light on the matter. What also suggests the authenticity of these fashion plates is the discretion with which so often only

[1] This remarkable woman, a housekeeper to George II, at Windsor, appeared at a masked ball in 1749 in the character of Iphigenia, 'So naked,' records Horace Walpole in his letters (ii 153), 'that you would have taken her for Andromeda.'

the tip of the breast and nipple is exposed. In such instances the nipples merely peep tantalizingly from either side of a scarf that modestly conceals the cleavage between the breasts (Plate 72). The crude and total exposure of the breast in English caricature suggests a convention in art, rather than fashion. Even the most revealing exposure of the breasts in French costume is still subtle, and curiously guarded.

That the English *décolletage* of the period was extremely daring there is no doubt. But this in itself is not evidence of complete exposure. There are many references to this style of *décolletage* in the writing of the day. In 1752 Arthur Murphy comments:

'The fashion is now to show as low as one possibly can.'
(*Grays Inn Journal*)

The very phrase 'as low as one possibly can' suggests that there was, generally speaking, a limit even to the most adventurous attire, and that the exposure of the breasts stopped short of the baring of the nipples. Even so, it was sufficiently provocative to draw the sharpest censure from the *Gentleman's Magazine*:

'As to the fashion of going naked-shouldered and open-breasted, in the name of decency how could it get a footing among the ladies of England?' (1753)

The condemnation is a key to our native hypocrisy, and to our xenophobia. In England respectability is an appearance; everything must look 'decent'. There is therefore nothing out of character in the protest of the *Gentleman's Magazine* which also hints that the shameful *décolletage* of the period must have spread here from some sexually depraved country like France.

But it is only the men who complain. The whore-hunting husband will demand a prim show from his own womenfolk. This is his cover.

In 1775, the *Lady's Magazine*, without moralizing, plainly comments:

'Stays quite low before, and the bosom much exposed.'

Englishwomen are fundamentally far less hypocritical than their menfolk.

However, in the absence of any English fashion plates which show the exposure of the nipple, as do those of France, we may I think seriously doubt whether Englishwomen during the eighteenth century ever did in fact wear their breasts completely exposed. All the documentary evidence points at most to a daring *décolletage*.

How prevalent was the fashion in France? Mr Laver relates it to high society. But other authorities are doubtful of the existence of such a fashion in practice. Miss Madeleine Blumstein, Research Assistant in charge of Costumes at the Victoria and Albert Museum, and to whom I am greatly indebted for many pictorial references, would not commit herself to any definite opinion. 'It's possible,' is all she would concede. Why then, in view of the apparent evidence of contemporary fashion plates should there be any doubt? The answer I think is that the exposure of the nipples was entirely a matter of personal caprice. In other words, the low *décolletage* of the period, edged with lace frill,[1] and with its wide base already laying bare a considerable expanse of bosom, made it extremely easy for the more saucy and coquettish women to pop their nipples at will over the foam of lace. They would have known presumably which of their male companions would have responded agreeably to such a delightfully seductive gesture. The nipples could have been returned to cover instantly. The theory is supported I think by those fashion plates which show only the tips of the breasts exposed, and more conclusively, by those which show a group of women in the same attire, some with nipples exposed, and others with them covered. The possibility is implicit in the style of costume, with its breastline of soft lace (Plate 72). Everything suggests that the practice of 'popping the nipples' was followed by some women, on some occasions. They could be exposed, or concealed, by the merest and speediest adjustment of the lace.

My own conclusions about the possible exposure of breasts among British women of the period is that, as so often appears to be the case in Rowlandson, the bosom may frequently have fallen out of the low *décolletage* in the general rough and tumble of an age celebrated for its bawdiness. But this would be a matter of accident rather than calculated design. In which event your chances of seeing an exposed nipple would have been considerably higher in low society.

Were the breasts ever worn fully exposed during the sixteenth and seventeenth centuries? Here again there is both confirmation and doubt. Rattray Taylor confirms the *espoitrinement à la façon de Venise*, and in 1588, William Averell writes of the women and the fashions of his time:

[1] This of course could also have been the frills or lace of the chemise.

'. . . the opening of their breasts, and discovering them to their wastes, their bentes of whalebone to beare out their bummes, their great sleeves and bumbasted shoulders, squared in breadth to make their wastes small, their culloured hose, their variable shooes . . .'

(*A Mervailous Combat of Contrarieties*)

It is of course well known that Tudor women exposed a considerable expanse of bosom, but did this 'discovery' include a display of the nipples? Contemporary references to the exposure of the bosom may of course have meant a baring of everything but the nipples. In 1617, only fourteen years after the death of Elizabeth I, the Venetian Ambassador records the appearance of Anne of Denmark, Queen Consort of James VI:

'. . . her bosom was bare down to the pit of the stomach, forming as it were, an oval.'

(*Venetian Calender:* Vol. XV.)

But the nipples could still have been concealed even within these startling terms of reference. It seems more than likely that had the Queen Consort's nipples actually been exposed, this fact would have been faithfully recorded.

I have been unable to trace any pictures of either Tudor or early Stuart times which show the nipples exposed in the fashions of the day. Yet one contemporary writer claims they were. In *Muffs and Morals,*[1] Miss Pearl Binder writes:

'Tudor women not infrequently wore bodices cut so low as to reveal the nipples, a fashion which recurred in the eighteenth century.'

But Mr Laver is more cautious. Replying to a recent letter of mine on the subject in general, he wrote:[2] 'What a fascinating subject. Curiously enough I have just been trying to answer a similar request about the exposure of breasts in Elizabethan times and found it difficult to discover any authentic documentation.'

Miss Blumstein has since advanced a plausible theory. She feels it is quite likely that depictions of the exposure of the breasts in Elizabethan and Jacobean portraits might well have been painted out at some later period. Perhaps under the Puritan aegis of the Cromwellian Commonwealth? Certainly there are in existence a great many portraits of the period in which the low-cut bodices

[1] *Muffs and Morals,* 1953. (Harrap.)
[2] 15th February, 1960.

of the women reveal nothing more alarming than a desert of flat white that seldom indicates even the basic form of the breasts.[1] Miss Blumstein's conjecture is the more intriguing since it could be proved one way or the other, by X-radiography. It would surely be worth examining a few such portraits in this way. Yet it does seem curious, even if she is right in her assumption, that no single painting escaped the censor's brush.

Mr Laver's objection to Elizabethan costume on the grounds that it does not reveal the form of the female figure adds yet another element to the mystery. The use of artificial supports, such as the 'whaleboned body', imparted a stiff and rigid appearance to the torso (Plate 75), in marked contrast to the soft and flowing lines of the Restoration period which made allowances for the natural form of the figure and clearly revealed the shape of the breasts (Plate 29). How, one wonders, in such constricting circumstances, could there have been any exposure of the bosom at all? As I say, the evidence, and the opinions of the experts are all delightfully conflicting. And the mystery, like all good mysteries, remains . . .

'Eye those rising mounts, your displayed breasts, with shameless art they wooe the shamefast passenger.'
R. Braithwait. *The Englishman and English Gentlewomen*, 1641
(*Handbook of English Costume in the Seventeenth Century*)

The problem of the exposure of the breasts in the costume of early Stuart times and particularly after the Restoration is rather less mysterious, and the available evidence would show I think that the nipples could have been bared, as in the late eighteenth-century French costume. The extreme *décolletage* and ample looseness of Stuart attire would have provided the coquette with every opportunity to display a nipple in the twinkling of a rake's eye. If this were so it would answer another doubt in Mr Laver's mind. At the end of the letter in which he comments on the lack of documentary evidence in regard to Elizabethan costume, he poses the relevant question:

'And did Lely's beauties ever really appear like that?'

The answer I believe is that they did when it suited them. But not as a matter of course.

So many of Lely's portraits of women embody the spirit of

[1] The *décolletage* might of course have been masked by a fill-in of transparent gauze closed round the neck.

brilliant and cynical licence that distinguished the reaction against Puritanism following the restoration of the Monarchy. As Sir Charles Petrie comments:

> 'Once the shackles imposed by the Puritan regime were struck off, both sexes began to take a delight in outraging the conventions to which they had been previously subject . . .'[1]

But Sir Charles is biased. He sees the perfectly natural reaction against Puritanism as a lowering of the standards of social life, and as the symptom of a general moral deterioration for which he holds the much mistressed Charles II substantially reponsible. Be that as it may, it is only in the second half of the seventeenth century that Englishwomen ever approach the arch-seductiveness that since this time has remained the prerogative of their French cousins.

Lely's delightfully sensuous art expresses both the literal, and the symbolic, voluptuousness of a glittering and frankly lascivious age. Often his portraits pull up just tantalizingly short of nakedness, to demonstrate that discretion is the better part of wantonness, and a primary ingredient in the sophisticated deployment of female charms (Plate 76). The spirit of the age which Lely supplements so brilliantly in his more saucy portraits, is nowhere better revealed than in a letter to the second Earl of Chesterfield, written by Barbara Villiers, later Countess of Castlemaine and Duchess of Cleveland. Her companion on this occasion was one Lady Anne Hamilton, later Lady Carnegie and Countess of Southesk.

> 'My friend and I are just now in bed together, and contriving how to have your company this afternoon. If you deserve this favour you will come and seek us at Ludgate Hill, about three o'clock at Butler's shop, where we will expect you, but lest we should give you too much satisfaction at once, we will say no more: expect the rest when you see, Yours, etc., etc.'[2]

The tone of the age is also entertainingly revealed in a newsy letter from Henry Savile, to Wilmot, Earl of Rochester. My quotation concerns Louise, Duchess of Portsmouth, a mistress of the king, whose great rival was Nell Gwynn.

---

[1] Sir Charles Petrie, *The Stuarts*. (Eyre & Spottiswoode.)
[2] Sir Charles Petrie, *op. cit.*

Whitehall. 17 December, 1677.
'My Lady Portsmouth has been ill to the greatest degree.
The king imputes her cure to his drops, but her confessor to the Virgin Mary, to whom he is said to have
promised in her name that in case of recovery she should
have no more commerce with that known enemy to
virginity and chastity, the Monarch of Great Britain . . .'

In such a bracing climate the popping of nipples would hardly
seem out of place—certainly not at Court level, and it was, after
all, only with ladies of 'position' that Lely was concerned. Then
we have the testament of Restoration drama which fairly hums
with bee-loud bawdiness. Against this popular background of the
comedy of manners, in which a pox is on everyone, and the men,
not satisfied with wives and mistresses, pursue the 'generous
whores' with irrepressible energy, Lely's saucily clad women,
many of high rank, display a most appropriate and dashing
coquettishness. If it was not altogether common for women to
expose their breasts as does Louise in one of Lely's portraits,
one has only to study the *décolletage* of Anne, Countess of
Shrewsbury (Plate 77) described as 'notorious for her beauty and
gallantries', to appreciate how simple it must have been for Stuart
'ladies' to practise the problematical exposure that was so
obviously, I would say, a matter of personal indulgence: an ardent
and seductive gesture for the right occasion. How smoothly, im-
perceptibly even, could Anne, with mischievous fingers reveal her
'rich rubies'. With what speed could Louise modestly reclaim to
cover her 'red rose peeping through a white'. The very acts are
implicit in the style of costume, and one wonders if Herrick was
not himself inspired by some such saucy display?

Lely demonstrates the maximum potential of the attire of the
day in the study of his wife Ursula, one of four simultaneous
representations in 'An Idyll' (Plate 78) which shows the artist
and his family. With her breasts completely exposed the painter
has depicted his wife as Venus. She also appears next to the artist's
two children, as an attendant maiden, and as the cup bearer with
her naked back to the spectator. The painter himself plays the
bass-viol.

How frequently during the second half of the seventeenth
century women of 'high rank' appeared in company with their
breasts completely exposed we can only conjecture. That they did,
and often, when the time was propitious, I have no doubt. Studied

89

in relation to the costume of the period, and the lascivious mood of the times, Lely's portraits offer, for me at any rate, delightful proof that for a brief spell Englishwomen exerted in their appearance a note of the sauciest sensuality—a coquettish convention that degenerated, alas, into the brutish vulgarity of the following century.

Correctly exploited, the sexual potential of fashion, at any point in history, is one of the essential tensions of the art of love: a spanner for tightening the loose nuts and bolts of a man's desire. When a woman adapts the broad principles of fashion to her own seductive ends she transforms a mere blue-print into a powerful, personal ally. Only by the extension or modification that a clever and imaginative woman can confer upon the façade of fashion, can it acquire the status of an art. And what art could exceed, in its sheer beauty, in its evocative potential, in its pure craft even, the appearance of the Countess of Shrewsbury? Even the curl of her hair is designed to lead the eye, helplessly, to the exquisite *décolletage* that hides, so tantalizingly, the sweetness of her breast. If the essence of art is the power to communicate a suggestion, and to evoke complementary responses in the spectator, then the individual adaptation of fashion is indeed a most potent art.

Today, while we are still in the throes of a sweater cult, the map of love is exploited, if less wantonly, by young women. The breasts may be more securely enclosed than in the seventeenth century, and less subtly insinuated, but their form is strikingly apparent. When they wish, women will always find the way to exert and exploit their sex and, combined with the long fashionable necklaces of the day, the form of the bosom is emphasized, as it was in the erotic art of India. The girls of the mid-twentieth century employ these decorative ropes of coloured glass and stone to the same erotic ends as did the Indian girls of the Gupta period. Now, as then, their primary function is to emphasize the form of the breast.

The exploitation of the sexual potential of the otherwise innocuous sweater by imaginative individuals, has raised its significance to the level of an art: the art of creating, through the personal adaptation on an impersonal fashion, an image of voluptuousness sufficiently strong to evoke the most passionate responses in the male.

★

But fashion is tension; the conscious insinuation of the erotic shapes, forms and spaces of the body. The more attractive the woman, the more intensely aware she will be of the part her ensemble can, and must play, in suggesting the desirability of her natural beauties.

However self-assured, however composed or relaxed she may appear to be, a woman dressed, as all women of attraction dress, 'to kill', is a woman dynamically aware of her every movement and gesture. While her appearance is subject to the scrutiny of the male eye, the woman of fashion will tighten every fibre of her being. Only when she has been conquered through love will she relax the hills and valleys of her body, permitting them to melt and flow, like spring snows.

Earlier I spoke of Renoir's portrayal of the surrender of a woman's appearance to the gaze of the loved one, and of how the heart of a sensitive and imaginative lover would dissolve in tenderness at the sight of the asymmetries and irregularities that present themselves in such moments of unguarded relaxation. But his heart will never be more deeply moved than when he contemplates the sleep-locked shapelessness of the loved one's body. Adrift on the ivory sea of sleep, a woman is, at last, utterly surrendered. Her breasts, flowing beyond sensual time and place, belonging to no one, assume the quality of soft hillocks washing away in a steady rain. Sebastiano Ricci's 'Venus Sleeping', although classical in conception, has conceded the asexualism of the goddess's abandoned breasts with an eye that suggests the reality of life, rather than a sterile convention of art (Plate 79). Likewise the drifting breasts of Poussin's 'Nymph surprised by Satyrs' (Plate 80). Here too, a master of the classical manner reveals his awareness of the anti-idealism of the forms of life. The asymmetrical and the irregular are the pillars of the order of nature. The ideal of 'regular beauty', whether propagated through art or fashion, is an illusion. But if desire is fanned by illusion, and curiosity stirred, the heart is only moved by the revelations of surrender. A woman asleep is a woman revealed. She is the purely and the truly naked. A man may desire the illusion of a woman's 'perfection', but in the end, he will love her only for her imperfectness.

And when at last, as in Rodin's *Celle qui fut la belle heaulmière*, the breasts of a woman, sere as the leaves of autumn, fall softly across the dry twigs of her body, a man of tenderness and vision might still say with Charles Cros:

> *I do not want to know what poles your mad orbit*
> *left behind it;*

THE MOONS OF PARADISE

Give me your breasts and shoulders;
Let me kiss them, and that is enough.
(From *Scherzo*. Charles Cros 1842-1888)
(*The Penguin Book of French Verse*)

He might say it, too, as he contemplates the sleeping breasts of a young mistress; for the sadness that links the images of youth and age, beyond the stations of time and space, is a reflection no less deep, and poignant, in whichever mirror we happen to gaze.

5

The Possessed

The madman and the artist are the truly possessed, although the possession of the artist by his demon is not necessarily madness. Neither has every artist a demon. When he has, his work will clearly display the intensity and the claw marks of his obsession. Michelangelo was possessed by the demon of anatomy, Rembrandt by that of chiaroscuro, and Turner by that of light. Lesser men may pride themselves on their addiction to alcohol, or tobacco, or gambling, but these are pigmy obsessions beside the matchless demons of madness and art. How closely the vision of the artist can skirt the kingdom of the mad we can see from the magnificent phantoms of Fuseli. His friend and contemporary Blake moved even closer to the twittering of the dark mansions. Some will have it that he entered the portals, but lacking the official pass of a painter like Richard Dadd, or of the poet John Clare, both of whom died in the asylum, the vision of Blake must in itself suggest what it will to the individual spectator.

There are, however, hauntings superb and commanding, this side of the frontier, that convey a clear picture of the splendour of an artist's possession by his demon. Of this kin is the erotic vision of Fuseli. Whatever roots the intensely personal quality of his vision may have had in the collective unconscious of his time—or may have in ours, for that matter—his conceptions were quite out of sympathy with the aesthetic *Zeitgeist* of his day. He remains, like Blake, the supreme outsider, flying the kites of his fantasy in the face of the dull and trivial realism that marked the official art of the middle and late eighteenth century. Few members have stood so remote from the conservatism of the

93

Academy as Fuseli, who was elected an A.R.A. in 1788, and an R.A. in 1790.

His eroticism, in which the breast plays a vital and obsessive role, is trimmed with idiosyncrasy and fetishism. The giant women who populate his fantasies, clad as Ruthven Todd puts it 'in parodies of the long clinging dresses of the period', their hair built into huge, elaborate coiffures, display an obvious obsession with the sexual allure of hair and clothing, and with the significance of these elements as symbolic of the sadistic potential of his *demi-mondaine*. These are the weapons through which they will dominate, and crush, and also punish. Fuseli's erotic imagery is naturally complex. The frank and simple eroticism of Indian art would be unthinkable in the context of a society which associates sex with sin, and the natural fulfilment of desire with guilt and retribution. In the West we are never far from the perverse need to convert healthy pleasure into unwholesome pain, as a penance for the naturalness of those lusts which produced in India perhaps the most cultivated and humane civilization in history. The desire both to inflict and to suffer pain is an inevitable outcrop of sexual repression. Where there is no pleasure, there must be pain: the infliction of pain upon others as a substitute for the denial of pleasure, and the suffering of pain as a punishment for the original desire. All this is neatly symbolized in the art of Fuseli, though he is not a detached commentator on the psychopathology of society as is Diderot in *The Nun*. Like Poe, he is completely involved in his hauntings. His art is not commentary, but symptom, and as such he is closer to Kafka than to Diderot. He is in fact the typical haunted artist of the West, impaled simultaneously on the horns of his own and of society's dilemma. Any statement of his personal deficiencies is soon encompassed by the wider issues involved. From the particular we are led to the general; from the malaise of one soul, to that of the collective psyche. But let us examine the situation more closely.

In spite of their evident intention to kindle the flames of desire, Fuseli's whores and procuresses remain wilfully remote and unattainable. Inspiring desire, they withhold its gratification. In personal terms they are obviously the mockers of the artist's sexual effeteness. Fuseli was a man of small stature and his women are immensely tall. This inequality of size symbolizes, I think, the painter's sense of sexual inferiority. The fantastic hair styles of his women, and the awesomeness of their clothing, arranged as

94

much to instil fear as to titillate desire (Plate 81) conspire to create an intensely erotic image, yet one malign, ominous and unapproachable. Stirring the fires of the most fastidious lusts, they stand, these giantesses, contemptuously aloof, fully aware of the desire they have unleashed but have no intention of gratifying. Only in the wanton exposure of their breasts do they appear to offer a prospect of love. But the oasis of the cool, refreshing breast is a voluptuous mirage flashing mockingly in the stony wilderness. The hair, the fancy-dress draperies, and the naked breasts scoff at the torment of the lover croaking in the hot sands.

★

'Think of Fuseli's savage and abandoned women—the daughters of the bawds of hell, engendered by demons.'
(The Autobiography of B. R. Haydon)

Haydon's comments are illuminating. Fuseli's women are indeed the daughters of hell, and their ferocity is aimed at the artist himself. The pleasure that Fuseli derived from the creation of his erotic type was evidently masochistic, for his women are essentially administrators of pain. They loom, ominous and dominating over the face of the male (Plate 82), threatening destruction, and perhaps even death. Was this threat of destruction what the 'little white-headed lion-faced man in an old flannel dressing gown'[1] desired most of all from woman? I would argue that the man who cannot dominate his women often desires to be dominated by them; and indeed often is. Fuseli's complex imagery rather suggests that his experience of women was primarily imaginative. Apart from his childless marriage, and a curious, sexless intrigue with Mary Wollstonecraft which was terminated by his wife, there is no evidence that Fuseli's sexual life was any more extravagant than that of the timid Mr Etty who it is thought, in spite of his passion for the female nude, may have died a virgin.

Fuseli's bizarre eroticism suggests, therefore, both an expression of, and a defence against, his ineffectuality with women. His sense of physical inferiority is symbolized by the overpowering size of his women, while he excuses his impotence by the implication that the fantasy of their accoutrements virtually insulates them from the advances of the male. Looked at objectively, the elaboration of their coiffures and the menace of their dress is a

[1] The Autobiography of B. R. Haydon.

95

THE MOONS OF PARADISE

defence against Fuseli. His demons are sufficiently externalized to live a life of their own, symbolic both of his and of the collective unconscious from which they also spring. Man, the individual, is inevitably the measure of microcosm, and macrocosm.

Yet even in the shedding of his demons, Fuseli demands to be dominated by them. He will be taken to task, and chastized. He must be made to suffer, to prostrate himself for flagellation before the accusing bosom and the raised switch (Plate 83) as punishment for his sexual incompetence and for the sinfulness of his desires. His chastizer wears gloves, symbol of her authority, but her naked breasts proclaim the dominion of woman's impudent voluptuousness.

Here then is the double image of pleasure and pain; the ecstasy of desire, and the penance of the scourge.

That such an image could emerge only from the collective unconscious of Christian society, with its fantasies of sin and retribution, is to me patent. Since the beginning of the Christian era it has been left to the individual artist to find symbols that will express the sexual tragedy of Christendom.

Throughout the middle ages this suffering was dumb, but in the late fifteenth century Hieronymus Bosch synthesized the whole field of medieval symbolism in 'The Garden of Earthly Delights' (Plate 7). The artist drew liberally upon the extensive iconography of his time. The toad and the pig for instance, represented the devil; fruits were sexual symbols; egg shapes and forms, symbols of fertility; oysters and clams symbols of the female.

The orthodox medievalist read this triptych as depicting Paradise (left wing), the sinfulness of the world with its unredeemed life of the senses (central panel), and the damnation and suffering in everlasting hell (right wing).

But a more recent interpretation[1] sees the central panel as the reunion of mankind with God through an ecstatic sexual celebration in which the whole of creation partakes, after the passage of humanity through the hell of the world.

Bosch is believed to have been a member of an heretical Christian sect known as The Adamites—Brothers and Sisters of the Free Spirit—who met in secret, and nakedness, to practise promiscuous sexual intercourse in the belief that unashamed nudity and erotic exaltation were an intrinsic part of the Creator's intention. This would seem the only point at which the Christian

[1] *The Millennium of Hieronymus Bosch*—Wilhelm Fränger. (Faber & Faber.)

faith and the Hindu concept of *Kama* are synchronized. But whichever view one takes, 'The Millennium', with its teeming symbolism stands as the greatest exposition of the sexual dilemma of Christianity in the history of European art. Fuseli's eroticism, though far less problematical, is none the less a continuation of the tradition in which the artist alone speaks for the community in this matter. Fuseli's whores, with their naked, tempting breasts, symbolize the menace of lust; not the divine, life-giving lust that illumines the erotic philosophy of ancient India—or of the Adamite creed—but the dark and shameful lust of the demented, orthodox West. Here the prostitute is associated with sin and guilt. She is devil and temptress. No longer the cultivated mistress and companion of civilized men as were the *hetairae* of Greece, or the courtesans of India, she stands in the shadows beyond the pale of 'respectable' society, wantonly plying her disgraceful trade, while exacting simultaneously her toll of guilt and retribution. (Although in recent times, to the consternation of the Church, the discovery of penicillin must have taken a lot of the wind out of the sails of sin, and its deserts.)

That our society is still far from adult, or civilized, we can judge both from the hounding of prostitutes by a new law,[1] and by the medievalism of a recent Archbishop of Canterbury's call to jail adulterers. The sexual dilemma of the West still persists, and it is this, surely, which forms the substance of Fuseli's erotic vision, overladen with the threat of domination and retribution at the hands of whores and procuresses. Did Fuseli personally desire the tyranny of woman's dominance? And in expressing the longing to suffer domination and pain at the hands of the opposite sex, is he not simply voicing the desire of the Christian male to seek absolution from sexual guilt, by setting responsibility for the temptation and the fall, squarely upon the shoulders of woman? The situation is only as complex as might reasonably be expected in the circumstances.

[1] Reviewing the book *Streetwalker* (Bodley Head) in the *New Statesman* (31 October, 1959), Peter Duval Smith, after commenting on the hypocrisy that is the English way in matters of sex wrote, with profound humanity and a burning hatred of hypocrisy—'It is now a couple of years since the findings of the Wolfenden Commission were made public, amid a chorus of male approbation. Perhaps the distance of time may lend "distance" in another sense to the bizarre spectacle of grown Englishmen complaining in the correspondence columns of *The Times* that strange women had been speaking to them in the streets of London. One cannot help wondering how many of these bold letter-writers have been accustomed to make use of prostitutes, and what their behaviour is with them. Partly through their clamour, hypocrisy is now entrenched by legislation.'

THE MOONS OF PARADISE

In a recent television interview, Carl Jung stressed the importance of not acting against nature. This of course is one of the primary causes of the degeneration of the Western psyche. We have been acting brutally and insanely against nature since the opening of the Christian era. Fuseli's art is symptomatic of the aberration of sexual personality which inevitably follows. The fixation of the artist's libido in fantasies of coiffure and dress symbolizes, therefore, not only the idiosyncrasies of an individual, but the patterns of social prejudice and psychopathology from which they spring. He is the truly possessed, expressing in his private hauntings the dilemma and the terror of the community as a whole. If his fantasies are sometimes close to the portals of hell, or madness, it is only the hell and the madness of a mistaken approach to the art of living. Such fantasies would be unthinkable in the context of the Greek or Hindu aesthetic where the breast is neither a synonym for sin, nor the perverse domination of woman, but the shape of all beauty and the fountain of all joy.

The surface of Fuseli's art appears unique, but the interpretation of his symbolism reveals the extent to which its roots are anchored in the collective unconscious. This of course is a feature of much Surrealist art,[1] and Fuseli was rightly claimed by the Surrealist movement during the heydays of the 1924-36 decade. Dali, Ernst, Chirico and Delvaux, each in his way appears as unique, only to reveal in analysis, as does Fuseli, the Freudian macrocosm. Only in this sense is the art of Fuseli an extension of his time. He leaves us no picture of the surface of an age, as do Hogarth and Rowlandson; his revelation is entirely that of the interrelationship between the personal and the collective unconscious. Fuseli's subject content has little aesthetic value. This is only evident in his technical style as a draughtsman. As a painter his style is dull and turgid, but his line is often superbly fluent and brilliantly searching. The rich content of his art is of purely psychological interest.

In 1765 Horace Walpole published *The Castle of Otranto* and set a fashion for tales of horror. Later, Anne Radcliffe, another exponent of the Gothic novel, published her romance of terror *The Mysteries of Udolpho* (1794). Because Fuseli is contemporary

[1] There are two streams of Surrealist art, notwithstanding Dali's insistence on the all-permeating significance of the Freudian thesis. There is the Freudian stream, and the lyrical, relatively asexual, and innocent visions of such Surrealists as Marc Chagall, who draw more upon the simple, involuntary memories of time past, particularly those of childhood, than upon the sexual repressions and complexes of adult personality.

with the rise of this vogue, the element of the sinister and the terrible in his own work is often, I think, wrongly construed as a reflection of the romance of terror as practised by the writers of his time. I feel this to be an inaccurate and shallow assessment of his art. There is little doubt that this extremely well-read artist was fully aware of all that went on around him. Yet the terror of the artist's vision, and the possession of his soul by the fantastic women who arose from the vapours of his mind, is the fearfulness, not of the romantic novel, with its many objective ramifications, but of a sealed and personal hell. Here the artist is imprisoned for ever, at the capricious mercy of his tormentors, like the characters in the hell of Sartre's *Huis Clos*. With coiffure, breast and switch to mock and chastize him, his damnation is subjective. But this again is only the private hell to which all the inmates of Western society have been committed for two thousand years.

Earlier I distinguished Fuseli as the type of the supreme outsider. But what is the outsider? To say that he is simply the nonconformist in a pattern of social and aesthetic conventions is to beg the issue. To begin with, one must realize that the outsider is essentially the product of a society in which the existing pattern of moral and religious convention is no longer above suspicion. The fierce scepticism and free thinking of the eighteenth century produced a rich crop of outsiders; Voltaire, Rousseau, Diderot, and even de Sade among them.

Even so, one must differentiate between the positive and the negative outsider. The one is a symbol of the community's reaction against the imposition of conventions which have turned sour; the other symbolizes the malaise itself.

Fuseli belongs to the latter category, Picasso, on the other hand, to the former. Both types of the outsider are possessed. Fuseli is possessed by his enslavement to fantasies of frustration, guilt and retribution; Picasso by his sense of freedom. If we compare Fuseli's 'Young man kissing a woman' (Plate 84) with Picasso's 'Nude on a Black Couch' (Plate 90), the difference is clear. The hot, parched assault of the man, and the sense of resistance in the breast of the woman, contrast sharply with the feeling of repose and fulfilment that illumines the Picasso. Here the breasts of the woman are not points of inextinguishable fire and torment, but cool fountains: the source of love flowing freely. Fuseli expresses the madness of frustration, Picasso, the universal dream of freedom.

The outsider, through his demon, reveals the two faces of the

99

collective unconscious; the yearning for freedom, and the nature of enslavement.

★

The ramifications of the sexual dilemma of the West are extensive and involved. Whereas the *lingam* appears unashamedly in Indian art, in the West, the phallus is admissible only in disguise, in the form of oblique and indirect symbolism. There would have been little meat for Freud if this were not so. I know of no clearer instance of the working of this principle in painting than Lucien Freud's[1] 'Woman with a Dog' (Plate 85). The artist's symbolic iconography, though relatively personal, is no less potent than the systematic employment of symbolism in the middle ages. In Freud's picture the dog represents the phallus. The hidden breast and the position of the hand represent the hypocrisy which masks the pure joy. Only in the naked, superbly sensual breast does the painter express his rebellion against the need for suppression. There is no symbolism here; the eroticism is frank and unashamed. But it is a frankness in conflict with the demands of hypocrisy. In this one painting the outsider has combined the polarities of the psychological dilemma of the West. The longing for freedom is opposed to the need for concealment. But the painter has much more to say than this.

Freud is possessed by the demon of minutiae. With a gift for *trompe l'oeil* unequalled in our time except by Dali, he can express the most potent and revealing meanings in a pin-point of detail. He can winkle the soul from a contour. Look at the naked breast in 'The Woman with a Dog'. There is no idealization here. It is the portrait of a particular breast. Its shape, form, contour and texture are as unique as those of any face. The contour of its form is irregular, and its asymmetrical beauty deeply touching. It is in no sense an ideal conception, but a fragment of human reality, the more poignant because of its frailty and defects. The painting of this breast expresses with microscopic tenderness the love of an artist's eye for that which is different from all else in creation. And is this not the very foundation of a man's love for the flesh of a particular woman. This is the face, the breast, the hand, unique throughout the entirety of creation, that is madness for one man. How moving is the painter's devotion to the exact character, to the littlest detail of the form of this breast. Every

[1] Lucien Freud is the grandson of Dr Sigmund Freud.

nuance of irregularity in the contour of the breast has been loved out. And why not? The pulse of love itself is an eye for detail. The lover who has not felt the hot tears rise at the sight of some slight, infinitely poignant imperfection in the body of the beloved, has never loved. One cannot love perfection, but the tiniest blemish can twist the roots of the heart.

'The Woman with a Dog' is a profoundly religious painting. To look is in itself an act of devotion, for in the miraculous diversity of creation is the revelation of God. Nothing in nature is duplicated. Every face is different, and every breast. The shape, form and contour of this particular breast is unique. To talk of the species of man, or of dogs, or the genus of trees, as though conformity to a pattern of broad characteristics were sufficient to describe the particular along with the general, is to pass by the essential miracle of creation; the differences of the particular within the framework of generality. Every fingerprint is different, every contour, and every personality. The moral and philosophical implications of this fact are clear. The intention of the life force—or God—is obviously a continuance of the principle of difference. A preservation above all, in anthropomorphic terms, of the uniqueness of man's personality, and of the goblet of the flesh that holds, for a while, the liquor of his spirit. God does not die-stamp his creations as though he were casting in metal or plastic from a master mould. In each case his modelling is unique. And so the sculptor, or the painter, in the uniqueness of his own technical style, each in his way approaches the intention of the divine.

Freud demonstrates the aesthetic application of the principle of difference. Morally our responsibility is evident. It is the differences between men that we must preserve and fulfil, not their similarities. The dangers of pursuing a realization of the latter to the detriment of the former has been witnessed too often in the past thirty years. To break man's uniqueness on the wheel of a political, or aesthetic, creed which dominates and finally destroys his right to act as an individual, is the true refutation of God. By his emphasis of the uniqueness of creation, Freud acts in the most deeply moral and religious sense. Beyond all specific symbolism, this particular painting expresses the depth of a painter's possession by the relevation of the unique.

Mithuna is one revelation of God; the uniqueness of shape, form, and contour, another.

★

While in England the outsider Fuseli was cutting his lonely and haunted path through the thickets of eighteenth-century reason and academic materialism, in France, an equally remarkable artist was at work. The sensuality of his vision intoxicates at a glance. The nun baring her bosom (Plate 86), and the woman lying across the sill of the dark window with her breasts spilling into the light (Plate 86), are overwhelmingly voluptuous. And what of the exquisite young temptress in the pointed archway whose eyes and lips speak the soft and thrilling words—*'Je promets?* (Plate 86.)

There is something so much more studied about these extraordinary conceptions than the haunted, seemingly involuntary visions of Fuseli. Their eroticism, though at first sight as complex as his, seems to have been far more deliberately thought out. Here one feels, as with Freud, is an artist who is the master of his demon. Fuseli was its servant.

'Et nous aussi nous serons mères; car . . !' (And we also, we shall be mothers; because . . !) says the nun, while the bird escaping from the grasp of the naked woman in the cavern of the window is covered by the remark—*'Il est libre'* (he is free). Evidently all these pictures are intended to convey a crisp message. But what? And why? And why does the breast play such a prominent part in each?

Jean-Jacques Lequeu was born at Rouen on September 14th, 1757. Until the revolution he was a practising architect of some note. During the period of upheaval he lost all his property, whereupon he promptly abandoned the profession of architecture to enter the civil service. To prove the genuineness of his republican sentiments in the days of danger, he produced an odd drawing titled *'Porte du Parisis'*[1] which was submitted to the Committee of Public Safety and exhibited at the Salle de la Liberté. Later, Lequeu wrote on the back of this drawing the remark:

'Dessin pour me sauver de la guillotine'

If indeed Lequeu's sympathies were genuinely republican, and there is no reason to doubt this, then his erotic drawings were almost certainly intended as satire, and not as mere eroticism. This interpretation would seem to be supported by the fact that all the pictures in question were drawn after the revolution. In her postscript on Lequeu,[2] Dr Helen Rosenau suggests that 'the

[1] The drawing represents a fantastic archway surmounted by a giant figure.
[2] *The Architectural Review*, October, 1950.

combination of the lurid and the sensual, the luxurious and the sensational' is comparable with similar qualities in the work of Fuseli.

I think the comparison is inadmissible except in the most superficial sense. Both artists are outsiders, both employ strange and compelling images as their vehicle of expression; but there the comparison ends. The art of Fuseli is concerned with the nature of psychological enslavement only so far as this is relative to the sexual life—or the lack of it—of the individual and his society. Lequeu, in spite of the superficial eroticism of his imagery, hits far more widely and expresses the desire for freedom and the nature of enslavement in relation to such forces as the corrupt and despotic powers of the Church, and the *ancien régime*. Dr Rosenau rightly infers the anti-clericalism of Lequeu's nun. In a single image the artist has brilliantly crystallized a tradition of anti-clerical satire which began with the *fabliaux* and *contes* of the middle ages, and culminated in Brunet de Brou's *La Religieuse malgré elle* (1720), and Diderot's *La Religieuse*, written in 1760 but not published until 1796, six years after the suppression of the religious orders in France.

Lequeu's nun might well be an illustration for Diderot's novel, in sympathy at least. In fact of course this could not have been possible since the nun was drawn in 1793, which is three years before the publication of *La Religieuse*. But the mood of the two works is thoroughly compatible and Lequeu certainly intended an attack on the convent system. Is there a possibility that he could have read an undercover copy of the book? Studied in conjunction with passages from *La Religieuse*, the similarities are so pronounced, and the sensuality so comparable, that such a theory can hardly be discounted. The breast is the most revealing symbol of all that womanhood entails, from the acts of sex to the joys of maternity. In the baring of her breast, Lequeu's nun might well be Suzanne, heroine of Diderot's novel, in the act of protesting against the denial of her right to the fulfilment of her destiny as a woman.

Many French writers of the eighteenth century, in their attacks upon the immoralities and the depravity of the various domestic orders, criticized also the monstrous endowment of nunneries by the wealthy parents of girls who were forced, for family reasons, to take the veil. Suzanne was one of these unfortunates.

'And we also, we shall be mothers; because . . !' Because what? This curiously cryptic remark might well be completed:

'Because we are women, and determined therefore, even if we are forced to bear illegitimate children, to fulfil our destiny.'

It was not, by all accounts, impossible in some convents to enter into illicit sexual relationships with men. But the core of Diderot's novel is the attack he makes upon the unnaturalness of convent life. In this context the breast is the flashpoint both of sadistic outrage and perverted sensuality. Lequeu's voluptuous representation matches perfectly the mood of twisted lasciviousness that distinguishes the activities of one of Suzanne's Superiors. But first let me set the general scene of the book.

La Religieuse tells the story of the youngest daughter of a middle-class family who is condemned to the hell of the convent against her will. Even her public refusal to take the vows cannot save her. After a scandal at the altar she is confined at home for a period, then again forced into a convent. Diderot describes Suzanne's experiences under a series of Mother-Superiors, one of whom persecutes, strips, starves, and actively tortures her out of the depths of sadistic mania. Part of her torment is to find her way along the pitch-dark corridors of the convent, her path strewn with broken glass. A later Superior seeks to seduce her into a lesbian liaison. Diderot presents a series of devastating psychological studies which are clearly intended to show the degradation of personality and the sexual depravity that must inevitably follow the suppression of all the natural and instinctive desires of life in the obscene atmosphere of the convent.

Compare the following passages from an English translation of *La Religieuse* published in 1797, with Lequeu's nun. Suzanne is describing her life while under the control of a manic-depressive Superior who vacillated between the extremes of savage punishments, and tender forgiveness. It was this nun who sought to seduce our young heroine.

'If a nun is guilty of the slightest omission, the Superior summons her to her cell, treats her with rigour, commands her to undress, and give herself twenty stripes with the scourge. The nun obeys, undresses herself, takes the scourge, and macerates herself. But no sooner has she bestowed a few stripes, than the Superior, having resumed her sympathetic disposition, snatches the instrument of penance, bursts into tears, laments her misfortune in being obliged to punish, kisses her forehead, her eyes, her mouth, her shoulders, loads her with caresses and with praises. How soft and white is her skin! How plump she is! What a lovely bosom! What beautiful ringlets! Sister Saint Augustine, how foolish you are to be ashamed! Let go that neckerchief, I am a woman, and your Superior. Oh, what a lovely bosom! How firm! Could I endure to see it torn by the lash?'

Bewildered, poor Suzanne comments:

'We pass from disgrace to favour, and from favour to disgrace without knowing why.'

Now follows two descriptions of the Superior's lesbian approaches:

'She cast her eyes downward, she blushed, and sighed; in truth, she looked like a lover. Then throwing herself carelessly upon me, as if she had been in a swoon, she said: "Hold your forehead near to me that I may kiss it." . . . I inclined myself forward and she kissed my brow. From that time, as soon as any of the nuns committed a fault, I interceded for them, and I was sure to obtain her pardon by some innocent compliance; it was always a kiss upon the forehead, the neck, the eyes, the cheeks, the mouth, the hands, the bosom, or the arms, but most frequently on the mouth.'

A scene at the spinet is even more revealing:

'After putting the instrument in tune, I played some pieces of Couperin, of Rameau, and of Scarlatti; in the meantime she had lifted a corner of my neckerchief, and placed her hand upon my bare shoulder, with the extremities of her fingers upon my bosom. She sighed; she appeared to labour under an oppression; her bosom palpitated . . .'

On the face of this comparison it is not difficult to reconcile Lequeu's conception with the spirit of Diderot's novel. As a pictorial complement of the prevailing mood of anti-clericalism, the artist's subtle and penetrating image is a biting condemnation of an evil system. By the very act of baring her breasts Lequeu's nun protests against the suppression of her womanhood, and indirectly, against the unnaturalness of convent life.

105

THE MOONS OF PARADISE

The artist is a commentator who uses the most subtly satiric forms to open up the long avenues of critical thought. One is seduced into thinking. His imagery is a scalpel laying bare the bones of contention beneath the mask of an appearance. In a series of drawings of facial expressions reminiscent of Lavater's physiognomical studies, Lequeu offers further proof of his analytical interests. Considered in conjunction with the methodical discipline of his training as an architect, there seems no doubt that his art as a whole is a carefully thought-out attempt to convey distinct ideas and messages. That he was obliged to present some of these under disguise is understandable considering the vicissitudes—often violent—of the period in which he lived. '*Il est libre*' and '*Je promets*' were drawn in the last years of the Directory when Napoleon was already plotting to seize power. For me, both pictures have a political message. What appears at first sight to be fastidious and *outré* eroticism is fundamentally, I feel certain, social and political satire cloaked in the form of erotic symbolism.

Dr Rosenau suggests that the caption '*Il est libre*' might mean he 'who escapes from the bondage of woman'. The soaring bird signifies presumably the recovery of personal freedom. But it could equally well mean the society which escapes from the tyranny of an oppressive political system. In which case the bird is the revolt against the *status quo*. One must remember that in 1798 the Directoire was on its last legs, and Lequeu would not have been the only sometime revolutionary supporter to play a turncoat for Napoleon. There is a classic example. In 1800, Jacques Louis David, who, by virtue of his neo-classical reaction against the frivolities of the rococo style and the patriotic nature of his subject matter, had earlier become the official painter of the Revolution, was now courting Bonaparte. In 1804 he was appointed *Premier peintre de L'Empereur*. But apart from a change of heart over political affiliations, David's style remained consistently austere, and his intentions substantially propagandist.

Lequeu's work must be related to the prevailing aesthetic mood which was established by David in the immediate post-revolution period, and which was to hold sway until Delacroix and Géricault led the romantic reaction of the 1830's.

'For him (David),' wrote Rene Huyghe,[1] 'more than for any other painter, art takes on the appearance of virtue. The hour,

[1] *David*. Catalogue of an Exhibition of Paintings and Drawings arranged by the Arts Council: 1948.

which Diderot waited for, has arrived. After the pleasure-loving aristocrat comes the utilitarian *bourgeois*. Painting must serve the dissemination of ideas and instruction.'

If Lequeu displays considerably more imagination than David—who cast this element from his art—there is no denying a comparative meticulousness of style. And although Lequeu's technical powers are much inferior to those of David, he is by far the more didactic of the two artists. The weight of his message is infinitely more subtle and potent.

'*Je promets*' might symbolize the unscrupulous ease and cynicism with which the state—and its spokesmen—will make expedient promises: promises they may have no intention of keeping even as they are made. Could not the two raised fingers suggest the double-facedness of political affairs? All political programmes are necessarily expedient, and as such, suspect. They can only be expedient since their ultimate fulfilment depends on so many imponderable factors: factors beyond the control even of the most well intentioned individuals. Once it becomes apparent that politics can achieve nothing, political life consists of the gradual corruption of good intentions and the transformation of idealism into a skilful deception of the people, on the basis of promises. The adroit politician will learn to conduct this cheating with an easy confidence. All this could be conveyed by '*Je promets*'.

Certainly the vicissitudes of political life in France between 1789 and 1815 leave no doubt that the revolutionary state is quite the most uncertain of all political organisms and one subject to speedy and violent change. Political affairs are not static, they flow continuously, sometimes sluggishly, at others with all the abandoned fury of a raging torrent. The personalities who elect —or who are elected—to try their skill in the river can agitate or cajole only in relation to the conditions of the stream at a given moment. They may seek, and indeed succeed momentarily, in creating the illusion of stability, but in so doing they will need to deceive the people with high-sounding promises.

The art of deception and double-dealing is of necessity a qualification of the profession of politics.

Lequeu is the outsider who expresses the longing of the individual and of the community to be free from the tyranny of institutions, whether religious, or political. He is possessed by the fundamental anarchism which is perhaps the mainspring of French thought and culture, and could account not only for the fierce radicalism of the eighteenth century as a whole, but also for the shattering of so many aesthetic conventions that were later to distinguish the violent individualism of the French contribution to the stream of modern art and literature.

One might even divine in Lequeu's curious and provocative art a first reaction against David's 'order', and a hint of the freeing of the imagination that was soon to follow in the rise of romanticism.

'*Je promets*' may well possess a double meaning in itself. It can satirize the worthless promises of the state and its rulers (the woman is presumably a whore and, in this context at least, a sign of the disreputable), or symbolize the release of the individual from the bondage of a society and its corroding conventions. '*Je promets*'; 'I promise to set free'. In this context the prostitute is a symbol of the sensuality which sets free the bird of the spirit.

In the pattern of a complex and guarded didacticism, Lequeu's most potent and telling symbol is clearly the breast. It can protest against the debasement of womanhood, it can symbolize the seduction of liberty, or the liberation of the spirit.

The work of Lequeu is virtually unknown in Britain and, his architectural drawings apart, hardly better known in France. The Cabinet des Estampes of the Bibliothèque Nationale possesses at least one volume of his drawings from which the examples of his work in this chapter are drawn.

Yet the impact, even of an odd drawing, is immediate and haunting. Having once made the acquaintance of his strange vision, the imagination is possessed, and thereafter haunted. This much at least he has in common with Fuseli; once seen, his work is not easily forgotten.

His satire is characteristic of French thought in the eighteenth century. Sceptical of authority, and possessed by the dream of freedom, he stands as one of the most interesting minor figures of the age of reason.

Malvaux's cry that 'All art is a revolt against man's fate' is the quintessence of the spirit of Lequeu's time, as indeed, of our own. For ours, no less than his, is an age of revolt.

The most devoutly possessed artist of our own time remains Picasso. None of the manias that have superficially enslaved his contemporaries read as more than passing enthusiasms—however momentarily illuminating—when compared with Picasso's devotion to the vision of freedom that has possessed him for more than half a century. The drift downward into the suffocating depths of theory, and the self-conscious, often hysterical, struggle to make a mark at any price, has marked the death of many artists of real talent. Choked by ideas that soon degenerate via fashion into mere cliché, countless painters have died on the cross of a spineless and affected 'intellectualism'. What else is the current vogue of abstract-expressionism? If an idea has no extension it soon asphyxiates.

Picasso's immense strength lies in the fact that he is not chained to an idea, but possessed by a universal force. His art shoots like a leaf from the branch of nature's continuous becoming. He is not a painter of ideas but of force. Whenever he has found himself temporarily shackled to an idea, as in 'Guernica', he has shed it, honourably and with all speed. Anyone who saw the remarkable film 'The Picasso Mystery' will have realized the extent to which the greatest painter of our time resigns the destiny of his being as an artist to the drift of the tides of the life force; to the embrace of the impersonal, pantheistic *esprit*. In accepting the miracle of the painter's role as vehicle rather than maker—it is only the little artist who self-consciously strives to create—Picasso reflects for us the pure condition of cosmic energy striking freely, like the sudden flash and crack of lightning from the palm of heaven. It is this tempestuous unleashing of the spirit of pure energy which characterizes the quality of Picasso's possession by the demon of elemental freedom. And just as the raging forces of nature inevitably manifest themselves in specific form, whether that be a storm at sea or a cloudburst in Snowdonia, Picasso never permits the forces that sweep from his brush to dissipate their potency in a splatter of fortuitous abstraction. He has never indulged in the aesthetic masturbation of *tachisme*.

Dylan Thomas expresses superbly the idea of the blending of abstract energy and concrete imagery when he writes of

> *The force that through the green fuse*
> *Drives the flower, drives my red blood*

It is only through the specific and tangible forms of nature and art that we can sense the rush and flap of the mighty winds that shake the halls of heaven. Picasso symbolizes the intrinsic freedom of elemental force, and to this end his imagery is directed. In his celebrated conversation with Christian Zervos (1935), the painter remarked:

> 'There is no abstract art. You must always start with something.'

He has never departed from this concept. In the face of the total destruction of the image by the later crop of his contemporaries, Picasso has always been aware that the forces which possess the artist can only be harnessed and brought into the context of human affairs through the body of the symbolic image. The dilemma, and failure of the *tachiste* is that he seeks to present the essence without the form. But Picasso writes:

> 'One cannot go against nature . . . We may allow ourselves certain liberties, but only in details. Everything appears in the guise of a "figure". Even in metaphysics ideas are expressed by means of symbolic "figures". See how ridiculous it is then to think of painting without "figuration".'
>
> (From the 1935 conversation with Christian Zervos)

Allied to this passionate awareness of the importance of the 'figure', or the image, is the intense pantheism of Picasso's iconography. Again he speaks to Zervos:

> 'The artist is a receptacle for emotions that come from all over the place: from the sky, from the earth, from a scrap of paper, from a passing shape, from a spider's web. That is why we must not discriminate between things.'[1]

The painter is the instrument through which the emotions of elemental force speak with vivid, symbolic compactness. The greater the artist the more willingly will he abandon himself to the tumultuous energies that press in upon him from all sides.

During the decade that saw the close of the twenties and the outbreak of the Second World War, Picasso explored the nature of the dynamic rhythms that sweep the female figure. Yet ideas are implicit even in the passion of his abandon. He is the most satirical and least sensual of draughtsmen. No painter of the nude has better appreciated the extent to which the ugly and the grotesque offset, and complement, the beautiful. He maps the hills and valleys of a woman's body not as so many erotic features, but as forms that evoke primarily sensations of weight, size, and movement. He delineates with frank and unerring satire the element of the ludicrous and the comic in the human form. He reveals the clown. But he also distils the force. The planets of the

[1] A. H. Barr. *Picasso: Fifty Years of His Art.* (Mus. of Modern Art, N.Y.)

breast, bouncing against the white flash of dancing flesh ('*Femme au Tambourin*': Plate 87) spring and jump with the force that drives the earth and sky, as the dancer's frenzy moves in exalted abandon across the black night of infinity. She is the timeless, placeless priestess of the rhythms of nature. She celebrates life. Her heaving breasts and buttocks, her flying hair and limbs, express the shape of the uncut energy from which society hews its subsidiary emotive drives. Love and hate and sex are all cut, according to the pattern-book of the time, from the rough diamond of primordial energy which springs, free and uncontrolled, in the fountain image of Picasso's dancer.

All concepts of beauty, every scheme of aesthetic ideation, necessarily attempt to modify the portrayal of this pantheistic force which, by its very nature, is unidentifiable with the supplementary ideologies of mankind. Picasso, who keeps this modification to a minimum, is therefore a painter neither of beauty nor of ugliness, unless we measure his depictions against some arbitrary concept. He presents us with an image of force, whereas, for instance, the Venus of Cyrene (Plate 2) expresses a concept of 'beauty'. Unlike beauty, however, force is not a changing and arbitrary concept, but an immutable truth.

The painter's image of force, 'Woman in an Arm-chair' (Plate 88) is ugly only by virtue of the fact that we approach the manifestations of art from the standpoint of preconceived and highly prejudiced conceptions of beauty and ugliness. Epstein is a modeller of force, and the charges of ugliness that have so often been levelled against his work are entirely the result of mistaken identity. The asymmetrical breasts in so many of his bronzes are ugly only if contrasted with an ideal conception such as that of the neo-classicism of Ingres. Once the artist, however impersonally, clothes the spirit in the form of the image, he automatically lays himself open to comparison, and then to attack. 'Beauty' and 'ugliness' exist on a lower plane than force.

Arguments about the relative beauty or ugliness of Picasso's imagery, especially in relation to the female form, are naturally inevitable, yet are quite incidental to his main objective, which is to liberate energy. Only as an aesthetic conception is the breast of a woman faultless. In actuality it is never 'beautiful' in this sense. Its form displays both the infinite subtleties described by Freud in his 'Woman with a Dog', and the incipient grotesqueness that both Picasso and Epstein express with such a remorselessly impersonal eye. Both artists are exponents of the grotesque

and the ludicrous, unless we feel the impact of their imagery as
pure force. I have heard Picasso attacked on the brittle ground
that his depictions are an evil and obscene travesty of the dignity
and beauty of the human form. Epstein has been attacked along
precisely the same lines. But anywhere, at any time, in buses,
streets, restaurants, trains, and certainly on the beaches of the
French and Italian Riviera we can study the raw material from
which the pattern of such grotesqueness is derived. It is in fact
far more the norm than any similarities which exist between the
human race in general and particular conceptions of ideal beauty.
But the grotesque possess a heart-rending poignancy. Picasso
knows, as only the most observant and passionate lover of women
can, that the body of the loved one is as ugly as it is beautiful;
that the breasts and belly and pudenda appear sometimes (and
of course always in pregnancy) as the preposterous antithesis of the
ideal. Reality is not the ideal, and Picasso, in caricaturing this fact,
makes it clear that if we must have an arbitrary standard of the
beautiful, then we must also accept the condition of ugliness as
its logical complement. And so, too, the lover must accept the
obverse of beauty.

The matter is discussed with amusing cynicism by the late
H. L. Mencken, in *The Lure of Beauty*.[1] The quotations that
follow are pertinent to the issues under discussion although they
lack the essential tenderness of the truly discerning lover of
women. Mencken is wholly a satirist and I doubt if in the last
analysis he really understood women at all. Nevertheless his
comments are relevant to our consideration of the nature of female
grotesqueness.

'The most effective lure that a woman can hold out to
a man is the lure that he fatuously conceives to be her
beauty. This so called beauty, of course, is almost
always a pure illusion. The female body, even at its best,
is very defective in form; it has harsh curves and very
clumsily distributed masses; compared to it the average
milk-jug, or even cuspidor, is a thing of intelligent and
gratifying design—'

★

'. . . it is extremely rare to find a woman who shows
even the modest sightliness that her sex is theoretically

[1] From *A Mencken Chrestomathy* and *The Vintage Mencken* compiled by Alistair
Cooke. (Alfred A. Knopf, Inc.)

capable of . . . the average woman, until art comes to her aid, is ungraceful, mis-shapen, badly calved and crudely articulated, even for a woman.'

★

'But this lack of genuine beauty in woman lays on them no practical disadvantage in the primary business of their sex, for its effects are more than overborne by the emotional suggestibility, the herculean capacity for illusion, the almost total absence of critical sense in men . . . A film of face powder, skilfully applied, is as satisfying to them as an epidermis of damask. The hair of a dead Chinaman, artfully dressed and dyed, gives them as much delight as the authentic tresses of Venus. False bosoms intrigue them as effectively as the soundest of living fascia.'

★

If we accept this argument, Picasso's 'Woman in an Arm-chair' is merely a caricature of an objective fact. Yet one cannot help concluding that while Mencken has seen, as Picasso has done, the element of the grotesque in the female form, he writes, as ofted did Wilde, primarily for effect; as for instance in Mencken's maxim, 'Love is the delusion that one woman differs from another.'[1] Had he written with true discernment instead of merely for effect he would of course have said, 'Love is the *realization* that one woman differs from another.'

If that were not so no man would fall in love more than once. Only the *forces* of life, love among them, are constant and unchanging in character. The outward forms of life, and even the character of personality which is an overgrowth upon the face of elemental force, are infinitely variable. Love is initially concerned with the individual forms of life, and is only later swept into the current of impersonal forces.

But if Picasso's "Woman in an Arm-chair' reveals the reverse side of beauty, his 'Nude in a Red Arm-chair' (Plate 89) summarizes with exquisite grace the charms of a woman. The breasts blossom like moons, and the lines of the body flow and mingle with a thrilling rhythm. Yet the image is still not fully sensual. The woman seems to be marking time on the brink of sensuality, awaiting perhaps a first smouldering caress to light the touch-

[1] *A Mencken Chrestomathy*. (Alfred A. Knopf, Inc.)

paper of her sexuality. The artist has captured here the moment of exalted purity before the quickening of passion, when the lover is swept by tenderness for the chaste loveliness of the breasts of the loved one. On the threshold of voluptuousness the head falls to one side like a rose, heavy with beauty. It is a moment of supreme wonder; a vision of the spirituality that suffuses a woman's flesh before the murder of love begins.

Implicit expression apart, the images I have chosen to illustrate a particular aspect of Picasso's art are basically images of force. The breast is a symbol of elemental, pre-sexual energy; a cold, mountain spring. It is not, as in the explicit erotic art of India, an image of arrived sensuality.

If one bears in mind that Picasso was a sea-child—he was born at Malaga on the South Spanish coast—there is in this fact alone basis for his life-long possession by the tearing gust of those essential forces that are closer to the dynamic patterns of the ocean than of the land. His restlessness springs from an inborn sense of the sea; of the openness and violent freedom of the ocean scene. This image has enforced itself continuously as a backcloth for his art. Even in subjects ostensibly remote from the ocean, the breast, freed in his vision from all sensual connotations, echoes the curve and roll and swell of the dolphin springing waves.

In his 'Nude on a Black Couch' (Plate 90), and 'The Mirror' (Plate 91), the painter has expressed with superb abandon the mood of this fundamental oceanic rhythm.

> 'I know from my own experience,' wrote the late Albert Camus, 'that a man's lifework is nothing but a long journey to find again, by all the detours of art, the two or three powerful images on which his whole being opened for the first time.'

Or to find, he might have added, evocative synonyms for the content of abstract force that articulates the forms of his heart's desire. The sea spirit that motivates a large part of Picasso's creative drive, haunted throughout his life that other ocean-born genius, the poet Dylan Thomas. He too strove ceaselessly to find again the first pure vision of his childhood sea, racing in to die away in a froth of shells and sticks and cigarette packets on the breast of the long shore that runs from Swansea to the Mumbles. To this image he is forever returning by 'the detours of art', as in the last lines of his poem of childhood, 'Fern Hill':

57 Renoir (1841-1919). Detail. The Bathers

58 Reg Butler
(1913-   ). Girl
Looking Down

59 Henry Moore
(1898-   ). Woman

60 Olga Jancic (1929-). The Lovers

61 Rodin (1840-1917). Le Baiser

62 Boucher (1703-1770). Venus and Mars

63 Rex Whistler (1905-1944). Illustration for Königsmark

64 Boucher (1703-1770). Diana

65 *right*, Claude Michel called Clodion (1738-1814). Cupid and Psyche; 66 *below*, Fragonard (1732-1806). The Bathers

67 Rowlandson (1756-1827). The Bum Shop
68 *below* Newton (1777-1798). Nymphs Bathing

69 Rowlandson (1756-1827).
Drunken Officer

70 Rowlandson (1756-1827). The
Landing at Greenwich

71 Rowlandson (1756-1827). The
Lovers Disturbed

72 French costumes and fashions. Late eighteenth century (1775-80). *Below* (1780-1785).

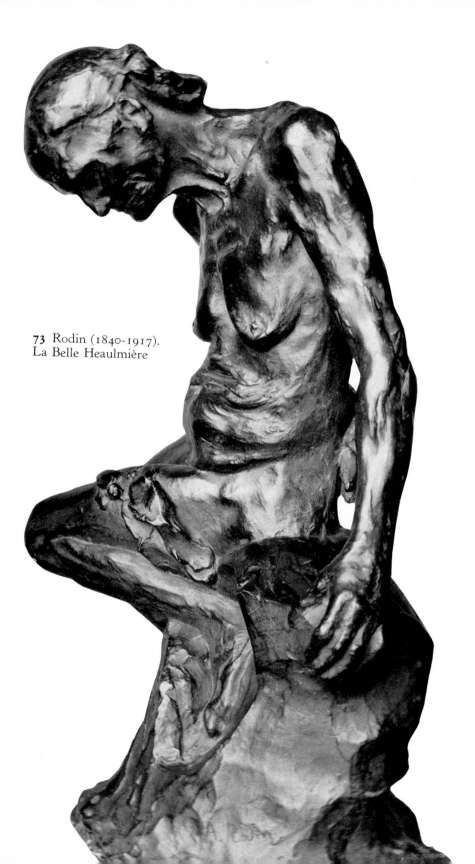

73 Rodin (1840-1917).
La Belle Heaulmière

74 Inigo Jones (*c.* 1573-1652).
Masque Costume

75 Queen Elizabeth. Artist Unknown

76 Lely (1618-1680). Nell Gwyn

77 *left*, Lely (1618-1680). Anne, Countess of Shrewsbury; 78 *below*, Lely (1618-1680). Detail. An Idyll.

79 Ricci (1659-1734). Venus Sleeping

80 Poussin (1594-1665). Nymph surprised by Satyrs

81 Fuseli (1741-1825). Three women with Baskets

82 Fuseli (1741-1825). Details from a series of
obscene drawings

83 Fuseli (1741-1825). Seated
woman with switch

84 Fuseli (1741-1825). Young man
kissing a woman at a spinet

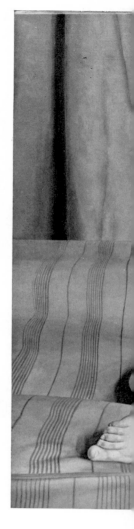

85 Lucien Freud (1922-   ). Woman with Dog

86 Jean-Jacques Lequeu (1757- *c.* 1829) *left* 'I Promise'; *centre* 'And we also, we shall be mothers; because . . .'; *right* 'He is free'

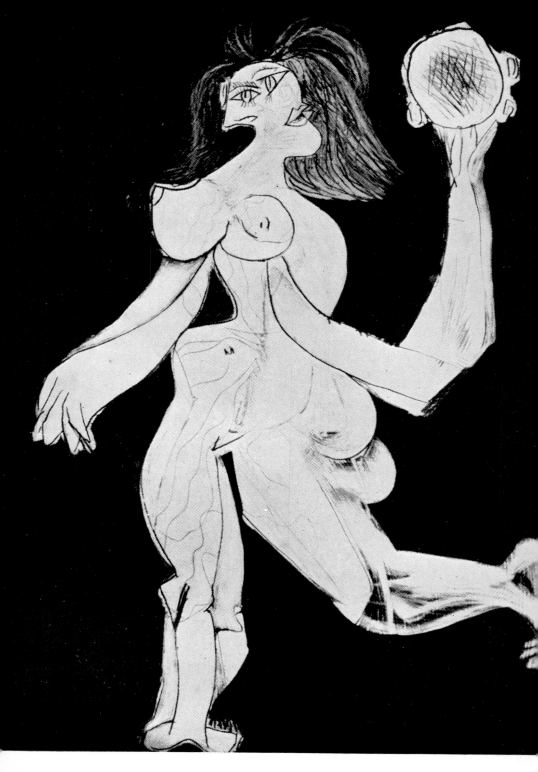

87 Picasso (1881-   ). Femme au Tambourin

88 Picasso (1881–   ). Woman in an Arm-chair

89 Picasso (1881–   ). Nude in Red Arm-chair

90 Picasso (1881-   ). Nude on a Black Couch

91 Picasso (1881-   ). The Mirror

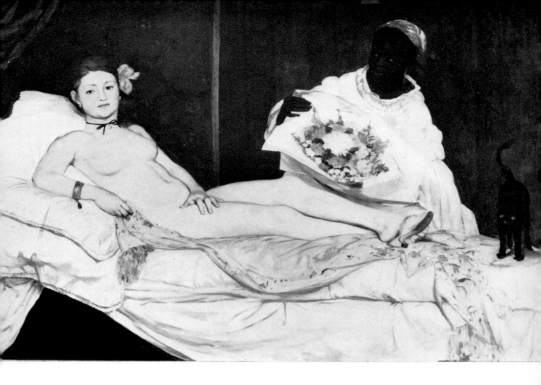

92 Manet (1832-
1883). Olympia

93 Marquet (1875-
1947). La Femme
au Divan

94 Clifford Hall (1904-   ). Back Street, Antwerp

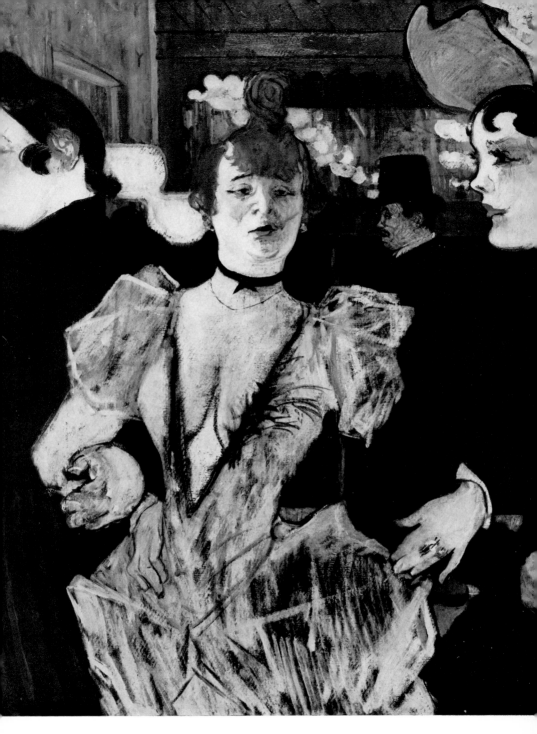

95 Toulouse-Lautrec (1864-1901). La Goulue Entering the Moulin Rouge

96 Toulouse-Lautrec (1864-1901). Woman adjusting her stocking

97 Pascin (1885-1930).
Two Girls

98 Chagall (1887-   ).
Lovers on a Horse

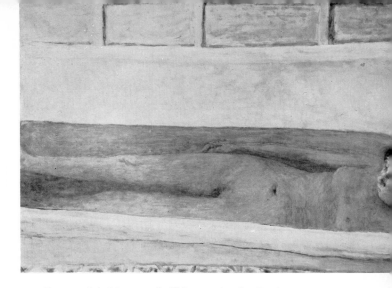

99 Bonnard (1867-1947). Woman in the Bath

100 Degas (1834-1917). Girl in the Bath

101 Dali (1904-   ). The Spectre of Sex Appeal

102 Beardsley (1872-1898)
Illustration to Volpone

103 Dali (1904-   ). Deta
The Resurrection of the Fles

THE POSSESSED

Oh as I was young and easy in the mercy of his means,
Time held me green and dying
Though I sang in my chains like the sea.[1]

But whereas all of Thomas' imagery is coupled with an idea, Picasso's vision of the breast in the sequence of illustrations I have chosen is one primarily of force, and only incidentally of idea. Here the breast is an ocean rolling, sea-springing fountain of pure energy, and only obliquely a sexual feature. The painter rides his brush over the canvas in complete freedom; he has no axe to grind, no message to hand out. If he is in revolt, it is only against the need to clothe the flood of his energy in any form at all. And is not the essence of force the fact that it possesses in itself no shape, whether we are thinking of the rhythms of love, or those of the sea? To make visible the invisible, this Picasso has done, though somehow reluctantly.

As the outsider he expresses the freedom that exists beyond the little orbit of any conscious human desire for freedom. Because of this his art is less in revolt than Lequeu's, less revelatory of the human predicament than Fuseli's, and less exploratory than Freud's. In the main he is not concerned with the human situation, and this above all sets him apart. Yet, in an age of acute and frequently misguided self-consciousness, this indifference is salutary, for until man, the individual, can see himself as element, rather than ego, he will never ascertain the true nature of his place and role in creation. I mean this of course not in any political sense, but purely in the sense that the ego limits the possibilities of our awareness of God.

In shattering the false idol of personal vanity, the painter has released us from the bondage of illusion: the illusion that being is an appearance. This is a common fallacy of the West, and since we put so much faith in appearances, Picasso's iconoclasm is naturally disquieting. But just as the Hindu lover strives for union with the divine by seeking to blend essence and substance in *mithuna*, so Picasso breaks up, or modifies, the illusion of appearances by submitting the substance of form, and gladly, to the force that crushes the personal in order to release the impersonal.

★

The four artists I have discussed in this chapter were not chosen for any similarities that exist between them—indeed they

[1] Fern Hill. *Collected Poems*, Dylan Thomas, 1934-1952. (J. M. Dent.)

are quite disparate—but purely on the strength of their intensity of vision. As outsiders, they each reflect in their own, unique conception of the female breast, aspects of the patterns of thought and being that stratify both the conscious and the unconscious awareness of man.

In the art of Fuseli the breast is a symbol of the mechanics of repression, in Freud it mirrors the uniqueness of the elements of creation. In Lequeu it is a banner of revolt, and in the facet of Picasso's *œuvre* that I have chosen for my own immediate purposes, it is an image of force and of freedom.

At the outset of this chapter I argued that the madman and the artist are the truly possessed, and if possession by one's demon is a symptom of madness, then the visions of art and those of madness are approximate if only in their intensity. Indeed one might argue further that the only thing which distinguishes the obsessive visions of art from those of madness is the artist's power to control, and switch off at will, the face of his hauntings. But the dividing line is often fine, and sometimes, as in the fantasies of Blake, or even Fuseli, distinctly blurred.

6

The Martyrs

'Nana was next to naked. She appeared in her nakedness
with a calm audacity, confident in the all powerfulness
of her flesh. A slight gauze enveloped her; her round
shoulders, her amazonian breasts, the rosy tips of which
stood out straight and firm as lances, her broad hips
swayed by the most voluptuous movements, her plump
thighs, in fact, her whole body could be divined, nay,
seen, white as the foam beneath the transparent covering.'   (Emile Zola, *Nana*; 1880)

Zola's vision of the prostitute Nana is as unrealistic as it is
indicative of the fascination which meretricious descriptions,
either in words or pictures, held for the English, and the French,
during the latter part of the nineteenth century. The more lurid
and obliquely lascivious the conception of the female body, the
more drastically it could hint, either in itself or by its juxtaposition
with other figures, at the idea of illicit sexuality, the more it
excited, secretly of course, the middle-class mind of the day.

The idea of woman as the tantalizing source of fleshly evil, as
the provoker and destroyer of men, was the absorbing theme of
the decadent writers and poets of the period. Salacity was insinuated, as in Swinburne and Bouguereau, through cloying
fantasies of allegory and allusion. It was essential, in order to
comply with the convention of outward respectability, that the
idea of sexual pleasure should be masked by some superficially
safe and 'decent' subject. Allegory was the favourite vehicle of
late nineteenth-century painters. But always, the onus for man's

descent into the chasms of erotic sin was safely humped upon the seductive shoulders of woman. Eve is not lightly forgiven.

'If women weren't devils, men might be angels indeed,' writes Willett Cunnington,[1] commenting on the masculine attitude towards women during the Victorian era. This is how Zola presents Nana.

In this chapter I am concerned with showing the different ways in which a group of artists have accepted the role of the prostitute in society, not as that of temptress, but of martyr, and how each of these painters, in his way, has used the image of the breast as the symbol of a martyrdom often borne with great dignity.

So as the more clearly to appreciate the nature of this martyrdom I have chosen the most perennial of man's sexual scapegoats, the common prostitute—not the élite courtesan—and by contrasting the far less romantic reality with the nineteenth-century fiction of the harlot as a beautiful and exotic siren, I have tried to distinguish between the lie and the truth. We are still sufficiently close to the spirit and influence of the 'eighties and 'nineties for this contrast to be effective. Indeed, in many ways, the sexual hypocrisy generated in Victorian times remains the measure of our contemporary mendacity. A recent item in the *New Statesman*[2] noted that 'about 36,000 plain plastic covers have been sold in Canada, mostly to office girls who want to read *Lady Chatterley's Lover* on the bus to work . . .'

One must remember also that the lying pornography of the late nineteenth century was offset, simultaneously, by the embarrassing honesty of Manet, Degas, and Lautrec, all of whom portrayed prostitutes with frankness. Against this relentless veracity one must measure the fallacy of Nana and the lie of a painter like Bouguereau. There is no truth in the once popular pornography of the French Professor. As Venturi remarks in his comments upon the artist's 'Nymph and Satyrs'[3] '. . . he suggestively painted the curved backs, the enticing breasts, and the rounded arms of the women. He prostituted himself, together with ideal beauty, in order to please people who lacked both ideal values and healthy sensuality.'

There is no warmth or blood, no humanity, no living sensuality in these frigid and sexless symbols of an age that sought to titillate its lust by proxy, and to sin by appointment with painting

[1] C. Willett Cunnington, *Women*. (Burke, 1950.)
[2] *New Statesman*; Critic. 28th May, 1960.
[3] Lionello Venturi, *Painting and Painters*. (Charles Scribner, N.Y.)

and poetry. The breasts of Bouguereau's women are a neutral reminder of the shape of true sensuality. In gloating over these globes of ice and marble the mind could cut its secret path to more authentic fantasies of lust. The pictures of such painters as Bouguereau and Cabanel are just dirty postcards.

In the same way the obscene lubricity of Swinburne, with its wine-dark hints at the sweet sinfulness of sex, complemented the mood of the time. 'The raptures and roses of vice', the 'furious embraces', and the bloody kisses that 'sting till it shudder and smart' are as remote from the reality of what it means for a woman to offer herself as a sacrifice for man's lust, and sexual hypocrisy, as Zola's fantasy of the whirling Nana. Swinburne's Dolores and Dowson's Cynara are pornographic phantoms.

In *The Second Sex* Simone de Beauvoir pinpoints the character, and the dilemma, of the real prostitute. In her acceptance of the degradation imposed upon her by man she is closer to the saints than to the creatures who defile her womanhood. 'The prostitute,' writes Mlle de Beauvoir, 'is a scapegoat; man vents his turpitude upon her, and he rejects her. Whether she is put legally under police supervision or works illegally in secret, she is in any case treated as a pariah.'

Did not man also reject Christ? And did he not by this rejection ensure the martyrdom of the Saviour? Rejection and martyrdom are the stones of sainthood, and of the saintliness of the prostitute. I can speak from experience. Far from seeking to corrupt and destroy, she is the passive recipient of the baseness man forces upon her. In herself she is often a woman of great dignity and morality. As a student at the Royal College of Art in the 'thirties, and a poor one at that, I was often treated to the price of a drink, or a meal, by Chelsea prostitutes, out of sheer humanity. I knew these amiable, good-humoured creatures simply as the most sweet natured and generous of human beings. Like Mae West they were not even remotely synonymous with real sexuality. They were too close to the realms of caricature and fantasy. Looking back, they appear in my memory as fat, ugly, often elderly, sad figures, rumbling with rough humour and subject to gales of satirical laughter. Only in their laughter did they seem to mock; and then, only at their pitiful and degraded clientele. They were, as I remember them, far closer to the bitter ideations of Rouault, than the exoticism of Zola or Swinburne. I recall in particular the vision of one of these ageing women walking towards me under the harsh, blue-green fluorescent lighting of Redcliffe Gardens. As she drew close, she smiled wanly, and with a few characteristic words, opened wide a cheap fur coat that had muffled her body closely from neck to knees. Beneath this garment she was completely naked. Painted in livid, fluorescent hues, she struck me, even then, as the living spit of a Rouault water-colour. Her shapeless breasts, the puffed and crumbling body, was the epitome I thought, not of sex and sensuality, but of that most pitiable ugliness, the ugliness of women unloved themselves, who must engage in endless fantasies of love with their destroyers. As she drew her coat close about her and passed on, I recognized the martyr—the rejected one whom Christ loved.

This is hardly the popular conception of the prostitute. For many, she still stands as a symbol of degeneration, and evil. A necessary evil no doubt, but one to be indulged secretly, and then vigorously denied. It is characteristic of the monstrous sexual hypocrisy of the West that our own Parliament has recently passed a law making it virtually impossible for the prostitute to ply her trade in public. Yet no one imagines for a moment that this is the end of prostitution in Britain. It is simply that man— and this is a man's law—cannot endure a public display of his necessary evil.

When Manet committed the unpardonable crime of painting a real prostitute, one still young enough to possess the rose of her beauty, but wearing already that air of dignity we can never forgive in those we ill-treat, France at once flew in his face. He was ferociously savaged. Fantasy was permissible; sex, obliquely insinuated, was tolerable because it could be mistaken for something else, but the truth, naked, and somehow accusing, this was unbearable.

In 1865, the French Salon exhibited Manet's 'Olympia' (Plate 92) and, already deeply shocked by the artist's 'Luncheon on the Grass' which had been shown in 1863, critics and public alike considered this fresh display of nudity even more intolerably scandalous than ever.

> 'What is this odalisque with a yellow stomach, a base model picked up I know not where, who represents Olympia? Olympia? What Olympia? A prostitute no doubt.'

This was the reaction of the critic Jules Claretie. But Zola, the writer of imagination who could visualize the lie of Nana, could

120

also perceive the truth in a painter of such immense integrity as Manet. He at once rallied to the painter's support.

'When artists correct nature by painting Venus, they lie,' he wrote. 'Manet asked himself why *he* should lie— why not tell the truth? He introduced us to Olympia, a girl of our own times, whom we have met in the streets, pulling a thin shawl across her narrow shoulders. But as usual, the public took good care not to understand what the painter wanted to say.'

And what did the painter want to say? He wished to accept the prostitute. He wanted to express the nobility and the dignity of a woman of the streets, still in the flower of her youthfulness, and with her calm, serene beauty, so gently spoken for in the proud carriage of her breasts, and the steady, tender gaze of her eyes. The orbs of her breasts are carried like the insignia of royalty. The prostitute who retains the dignity and pride of womanhood is naturally the most hated of her kind. For this reason alone Olympia was loathed. Her breasts are celestial badges. In this slip of a girl there is no hint as yet of the decay which Lautrec revealed in his studies of prostitutes. The martyr has not so far been too badly savaged by society. It is a conception that contrasts strikingly with Albert Marquet's '*La Femme au Divan*' (Plate 93). Here the painter has caught the razor cynicism of the eyes, and the calculating slash of the mouth. It compares with many of Lautrec's portrayals. The breasts are beginning to sag under the stress of that physical martyrdom which culminates in the terrible imagery of Rouault. The sense of physical decay is imminent. Of spiritual and moral dissolution only God can know.

Manet's 'Olympia' is perhaps the most dignified and moving portrayal of a young prostitute ever set down by a painter. Only the wistful child prostitutes of Pascin can be compared with the French painter's magnificent evocation. As do Pascin's tremblingly beautiful manifestations, Olympia transcends the limits of personality. She is not so much a portrait of Manet's favourite model, Victorine Meurend, as a symbol. The ivory nobility of her full breasts, as perfect in form as any late Greek or Renaissance conception, are still remote from the defiling touches of her clients. She is the peerless, inaccessible woman; Christ's loved one, whom no man, save in the mutual exchange of true love, could ever possess. She will be martyred, but she will never be owned.

THE MOONS OF PARADISE

It is this quality of inviolate apartness, expressed here so well in the aloofness of the young woman's breasts, that can impart to the martyrdom of the prostitute the perceptible aura of divine grace.

But Rouault is not concerned with beauty or dignity; only with ugliness. In his monograph on Rouault,[1] James Thrall Soby includes a section of comments on the artist's paintings of prostitutes in which he says:

> 'It is significant that many of the pictures which in-augurated Rouault's personal style should have reflected the frenzied preoccupation with sin and redemption ex-pressed in Bloy's 'Le Désespéré' and 'La Femme Pauvre'. It seems likely too, that Rouault's choice of prostitutes as symbols of earthly degradation—and also as subjects for instant redemption through suffering—was inspired by Bloy. Prostitutes had played a part in Bloy's writing and life. He had loved and converted to his own passion-ate Catholicism two women of the streets, later used as heroines in his novels. In Bloy's novels, prostitutes are the absolute counterparts of saints, and he made it abundantly clear that he was interested only in extremes of conduct and character . . .'[2]

And then, in a paragraph which pinpoints brilliantly the apo-theosis of Rouault's vision, he goes on to say:

> 'A relation between these water-colours and Lautrec s art has been mentioned by several critics. But few of Rouault's early paintings show the sensual relish of decadence for its own Satanic sake which characterized Lautrec's work. To Lautrec's cynicism, Rouault opposed tears and rage. He was not interested in the detailed decline of the flesh which so inevitably fascinated the crippled Lautrec. He sought the grimace and posture of irrevoc-able martyrdom. And he himself has indignantly denied the influence of the Degas-Lautrec tradition . . . "It was not the influence of Lautrec, Degas or the moderns which inspired me, but an inner necessity and the perhaps unconscious desire not to fall full-length into conventional religious subject matter." '

[1] James Thrall Soby, *Georges Rouault*. (Mus. of Modern Art, N.Y.)

[2] Rouault, a friend of Léon Bloy was deeply influenced by the Catholic writer's insistence that art and religion are inseparable. Bloy envisaged the function of art as the creation of a system through which one could display the ugliness and de-gradation of evil. Of Rouault's art André Suarès wrote: 'You paint as one exorcises.'

In Rouault's portrayals of prostitutes we can study the genesis of perhaps the greatest religious painter of our time. It is significant that the artist should have selected such an unlikely vehicle through which to convey the nature of his religious awareness and conscience. Most artists with an interest in religious subjects are instantly beguiled by the grandiose possibilities of such aspects of the Christian story as the Crucifixion, the Resurrection, or the Descent from the Cross. But Rouault, who during the years 1903-1904, had sought a more oblique symbol of the meaning of human suffering, found it in the person of the prostitute. Evil and degradation and the prospect of redemption through the martrydom of the flesh—was not Christ's flesh martyred at the hands of men?—this is the message of that phase of Rouault's art we are at present considering. Lautrec who was in no way concerned with the moral or religious implications of ugliness could view the decay of the flesh with an eye for its objective and impersonal beauty. For him, the breast was not a moral configuration, but a shape, and a form, that could appear as aesthetically beautiful even in the most degenerate or decadent context. To Yvette Guilbert he once remarked:

'Always and everywhere, ugliness has its accents of beauty—the thrill is to reveal them where no one else notices them . . .'

This coldly detached and, by the standards of Bloy or Rouault, amoral, or even immoral concept, compares sharply with the philosophy of Ernest Hello, another Catholic writer whose influence upon both Bloy and Rouault was marked. He wrote:

'Art is one of the forces which have corrupted the imagination because art has said that evil was beautiful. Art must be one of the forces which cure the imagination; it must say that evil is ugly '[1]

Whether or not in this argument Hello was attacking the art of such painters as Lautrec, there seems no doubt that Rouault, in his pictures of the martyrdom of the prostitutes' flesh, has deliberately set out to show, as Hello advised, only that evil is ugly. As an expressionist, his distortions have made full use of their power to imply the moral considerations underlying the face of ugliness. Particularly that ugliness which springs from the self-imposed degradations of mankind.

[1] Ernest Hello, L'Homme, 1936.

THE MOONS OF PARADISE

In his studies of prostitutes (Plate 54), we are confronted with the appalling truth. The dry, shapeless breasts are the measure of women's martyrdom. By nature the badge of beauty and love, they are here the object of corruption and shame. And yet, in the shadow of this horrific martyrdom exist the seeds of redemption. For the gutter is not infrequently a springboard to the stars. The ugliness of these tragic figures mirrors the face of the evil that created their decrepitude, and the destruction of the line, shape and form that we associate with the physical patterns of love—such as Rodin expressed in 'Le Baiser', with its perfection of aesthetic grace. Love transfigures; and even lust, as an integral facet of divine love, can raise the lovers into the high halls of paradise. But lust unshared is the soil of dissolution. Because it is egotistical and self-seeking it is sterile and rooted in the dust. The client and the prostitute alike partake of the bitter bread of a sterile pact. Both are degraded by an act which can only ennoble, and transfigure, if it is mutually enjoyed. Thus Rouault's terrible vision of the prostitute's breast is a moral comment. He says that the martyrdom of woman in these circumstances is evil and ugly and a crime against the concept of love as a divine union of mutual revelation and fulfilment. Rouault sees the breast with a moral eye; Marquet as a reporter stating a fact. There is no implied comment, no moral indignation, merely straightforward reportage.

The British painter Clifford Hall has also reported on the appearance of the prostitute. Her martyrdom is incidental to his view, and yet, in the very stance and posture of his women (Plate 94) in the resignation of their eyes, of their whole being, we are aware of the martyrdom of the rejected ones. 'Back Street, Antwerp' is one of a series of pictures of Belgian prostitutes which Hall painted a few years ago. The woman with the low cut dress is brazenly exposing just sufficient of her breasts and their cleavage to stimulate desire in prospective clients. Visually, one is reminded of a description of the breasts of a whore by Gerald Kersh. He likens them to 'chamber-pots'. Even so, there is no sense here of the degradation of Rouault's imagery. This may be implicit in Hall's ideations, but it is not immediately apparent. Nor is it a primary consideration, as it was with Rouault. Indeed, there is much dignity, and beauty too, in the carriage of the standing figures, and the faces of the women. They are hardened professionals, yet they are not without attractiveness. Is this the evil beauty against whose bewitchments Hello was so anxious to warn the painter? But such considerations are perhaps in-

124

cidental. It is amoral reportage, brilliantly observant, and coldly dispassionate. Yet there is beauty here; the beauty of *décolletage* which, detached from all subject considerations remains as perennial a feature of the art of seduction as the use of perfume, or any of those subtle accessories, or coquetries of attire, which women have always employed to enchant and enslave men. The tragedy is that where women would naturally prefer to exert these bewitchments in the cause of a mutual and genuine love, men have forced upon them, in the form of prostitution, the need to apply their sexual imagination as an economic device. Nevertheless, there remains the eternal Blazes Boylan, forever looking into the blouses of women, as well he might here, for the sweet joy of it:

> 'The blonde girl's slim fingers reckoned the fruits.
> Blazes Boylan looked into the cut of her blouse . . .
> Bending archly she reckoned again fat pears and blushing peaches.
> Blazes Boylan looked in her blouse with more favour . . .'[1]

★

Unlike the impartial reportage of Marquet and Hall, Lautrec's documentation of the prostitute is extended by a vein of pure cynicism which patently delights in the dissolution of the flesh. There is no salacity, only a cold, clinical analysis of the aesthetic qualities of decay. The moral significance of the martyrdom of the body had no meaning for Lautrec. Where Rouault would have construed the droop of an eyelid, or the sag of the breast, as moral issues, Lautrec took pleasure in delineating for its own sake the beauty which is inherent in all physical ugliness. The beauty of line, shape and form, in divorce from the story-telling subject. And if, in emphasizing these characteristics Lautrec should happen—as he invariably did—to heighten and intensify his presentation of character, that merely gave a double edge to the razor of his view. La Goulue, Yvette Guilbert, May Belfort and Jane Avril were all stripped naked to their souls by this remorseless process of arriving at a statement of character. Lautrec worked from the particular to the general; from those points of maximum dissolution that were the key to a personality. From the beauty of ugliness he constructed the essence of character. 'La Goulue Entering the Moulin Rouge' (Plate 95) is a magnificent example of the way in which this process works out. The angle of the

[1] James Joyce, *Ulysses*. (J. Lane.)

eyebrows and the droop of the eyelids are the focal point of the weariness that tracks debauchery; the curl of the mouth suggests the contempt which the prostitute may justifiably feel, and which is her main defence and vengeance against the society that has sacrificed her womanhood. It is interesting to reflect, looking at this portrait, how the polarities of sacrifice to which society subjects its women, the nun on the one hand and the prostitute on the other, tend equally to neutralize sexuality. In the last analysis the whore is as sexless as the nun. Both are martyrs; the one in the name of God—the other in that of man.

The measure of La Goulue's martyrdom is neatly implied by Lautrec in the ruin of her breasts, seen here in a gown that recalls the fashions of Tudor England. They are flat, shapeless appendages, hanging like dough beneath the flimsiest of garments. The beauty of the two, long, sweeping lines that demarcate the inner boundaries of these decrepit forms, tells at once the story of a life lived on the level of the brute senses. Yet, in themselves, the magnificent, ascending sweep of these contours, rising to their crescendo in a sharp pinnacle, might have been etched by the hand of Apelles.

Coarse, greedy and drunken, La Goulue died as a charity patient at the Lariboisière Hospital in 1929. From the delineation of these three points of reference, the eyes, the mouth and the breasts, each beautiful when studied in detachment from the subject, the painter has laid naked the soul of his character, as a surgeon would lay bare the form of a cancer.

The same frank description of the breasts in his study of a 'Woman adjusting her Stocking' (Plate 96) qualifies the sacrifice of the prostitute by virtue of the indifference with which the woman exposes herself to the artist's enquiring eye. It is thus that a woman will abandon the sight of herself to a lover, or a husband (less likely perhaps!), but not, unless she is a professional, to a stranger. In this latter role she will have ceased to care *how* she looks, because she will know that the desires of men are titillated as much by chance as by design. Herrick was well aware of this when he wrote: 'A sweet disorder in the dress, kindles in love a wantonness.'

And since it is upon the stimulation of transient lust that the prostitute relies for her livelihood, she is trained to relinquish instinctively, as here, the discreet concealment of her body that a woman will normally exercise in the presence of any man, other than a lover.

Only the martyr to love, or as here, to vice, is careless of her appearance in the company of men. The mistress because she knows, that no matter what blemish or defect she may in fact possess, it will be masked by the blind passion of her lover; the whore, because she will know that an abandoned *déshabillé* is one of the most sexually stimulating of devices.

The blobs of flesh which Lautrec has noted with such little ceremony are the breasts of the martyr. He pays them no homage. He neither dotes on their 'perfection' as did the Greeks and the masters of the Renaissance, nor does he see them as elements in the pattern of an erotic mystique such as that which absorbed the artists of classical India. In emphasizing their insignificance, the artist has shown the tragedy of the woman who, in the service of 'love', must suffer the shaming of her flesh and the desolation of her pride. In short, she no longer cares.

The proud, plump apples of the classic mould, the great moons of Indian erotic art, are the emblems of a woman's beauty. The shapeless pancakes and bags of the prostitute's breasts are the symbol of her martyrdom.

★

The art of the nineteenth century is a major cross-road in the appearance of the female breast in painting and sculpture. On the one hand there is the asceptic classicism of Ingres which soon degenerated into the slick pornography of the Paris Salon and the Royal Academy; on the other, the new trend in realism, established by Manet, and continued by Lautrec and Degas. The portrayal of real, flesh-and-blood women, in the ordinary, unclassical attitudes of boudoir and bathroom, was their contribution to this, at the time, alarming new direction. Tentative at first in Manet, satiric and cynical in Lautrec, the new realism gradually settled down until, in the vision of Degas, and later Bonnard and Sickert, the nude was painted with no more fuss or ceremony than an artist would make of a dish of apples.

Gone at long last were the sexual taboos; cleansed of the myths of sin, and classicism, and the mystique of nineteenth-century pornography, the female nude became an ordinary, everyday, matter-of-fact subject for the painter. This is how Jules Pascin looked upon the world of prostitutes that absorbed his attention as completely as it had engaged the interest of Lautrec. But there was a difference. Where Lautrec had seen only corruption and decay, Pascin discerned a tender, wistful sadness in the martyrdom of his young girls. They are little more than children and, as yet, scarcely aware of the immensity of the sacrifice they will be compelled to make. In this gathering gloom Pascin miraculously preserves the quality and character of childhood. Looking at his young girls with their breasts hardly formed, one feels that for them, the world of vice is still a children's game.

On Thursday, June 5th, 1930, Pascin, ill and despondent, hanged himself. Although still a comparatively young man—he was born in 1885—the artist, exhausted by alcohol and other excesses, could no longer endure the patterns of vice from which he had sucked the substance of his inspiration. Pascin is not a great painter. He possessed neither the insight of Lautrec, nor the substance of Degas. He pushed the real world close to the portals of dreams; of dreams and reveries into which his characters sink, seeking refuge from the brutish clamour of evil.

To the depiction of his young prostitutes he brought a delicacy of draughtsmanship, trembling, and nervous, that distilled the poignancy of their gentle abandon. For these young women Pascin must have felt deeply. He drew and painted them with love and humility, and at his touch they were transfigured. His children are the little saints of the brothel, slumbering in the soft reaches of their unassailable innocence. Where Rouault had seen only the ugliness of evil, Pascin divined the inviolate beauty of youth that no evil can touch or sear. In their martyrdom he saw the young prostitutes of Paris carrying their breasts like nosegays at the funerals of love; bearing like bridesmaids the sacrificial flowers of their youth and beauty to be trampled on the altars of darkness. And yet, these youthful martyrs are out of reach; they sit, and lie, quietly, on the other side of time (Plate 97), so sweetly abandoned, beyond ugliness, or evil, or morals. In their immense purity the blossoms of their breasts rise phoenix-like from the debris of childhood, so lately shattered by the stones of the adult world, with its creeping paralysis of vice, hypocrisy, and decay.

In his preface to Horace Brodzky's book on Pascin[1] James Laver suggests that the artist's girls are not so much individuals, particular persons, as 'universal types'. I think he is right; behind the stark fact that these wistful children were also prostitutes is hidden the more significant truth, that childhood, and early youth, possess their own unprofaned character, a marvellous apartness, wrapped in dreams, and often melancholy, that the corrupted mind of adulthood can neither understand, nor convert to its

[1] Horace Brodzky, *Pascin.*

own debasement. Pascin's girls are as much symbols of youth as pictures of prostitutes. The flowers of their breasts are a reminder of what is lost when we cross the bridge from the morning of childhood and youth into the night-time of mature years.

The quotation which follows crystallizes not only the difference between Pascin's vision and that of Lautrec, but also the character of the painter's 'universal type'.

'The world which Pascin chose, as by a natural instinct, was the world of Paris at midnight. It was the same world as that of Toulouse-Lautrec, but how different was the resulting vision. On the one hand we have the angular outline, the wilfully harsh yet miraculously blended colour, the flat, deliberate decorative scheme, the pitiless eye of the aristocratic dwarf; on the other a passive, Oriental acceptance, a flowing, evanescent colour, a fugitive line, and a tenderness which is the more moving because it never once lapses into senti-mentality. Lautrec might live in a brothel, but he was never of it. His vision remains a criticism. In Pascin there is no hint of criticism at all. He sought the company of *"les filles de Montparnasse"* because he felt at home in their company, and he felt at home with them precisely because they had abandoned their sheet-anchors, thrown over whatever conscious intelligence they had ever had and were pure creatures of instinctive reaction. They belonged to that "world of water" of which Jung speaks, where the individuality is no longer "capsulated", separate, distinct. So there is no *character* in his figures, no later equivalents of *Grille d'égout* and *Nini-patte-en-l'air.* His girls are scarcely individuals at all, and that not because they are superficially observed but because they are so profoundly observed. They belong to the world of the undifferentiated, and acquire the importance and the dignity of universal types.'[1]

Pascin's melting, and dreamlike vision of the breasts of his young prostitutes balances perfectly Laver's likening of these tender creatures to Jung's 'world of water . . .'

[1] James Laver: Introduction to *Pascin*, by Horace Brodzky. (Nicholson & Watson.)

7

Private View

'. . . and then I asked him with my eyes to ask again
yes and then he asked me would I yes to say yes my
mountain flower and first I put my arms around him yes
and drew him down to me so he could feel my breasts
all perfume yes and his heart was going like mad and
yes I said yes I will yes.'   James Joyce—*Ulysses*

'All naked all naked, your breasts are more fragile than
the perfume of frozen grass and they support your
shoulders. All naked.'   Paul Eluard—*Shared Nights*

★

Scratch the public face, scrape away the muck of lying and cheating, and you will find in reverie, and dreams, the private view.
Beneath the face that we all prepare, with Mr Eliot, to meet the
faces that we meet, is the eye of the poet, glittering with fireflies.
Mrs Bloom's soliloquy, Paul Eluard's piercingly sweet vision, and
Chagall's dream of ecstasy rising on the pink balloons of the
beloved's breasts, are all of them one side of the medal of the
private view. The real face of the unreality of our being. These
are the dreams that start deep in the reflective brows of the
women, floating in their baths, combing their hair, or sponging
their backs, in the canvases of Bonnard and Degas. The moment
of reflection, concentrated, compact, brilliantly focused in the
lens of musing, this is the condition of being that absorbs so
much of our life. The best and the worst that we are, is buried
under the pack-ice of our past. We live only momentarily a life

of flesh and blood; eating, loving, hating, working, dying. With each day that we add to the snowball of the past that is all we are, we rely more and more on reflection, and dreaming, for the substance of our existence. How is this fact demonstrated in the pictures of the breast that I have used to illustrate this chapter? Through the poetry of its fixed, trance-like aspect. As a symbol of the poetic relaxation through which we achieve eternity, in dreams, or recreative reflection. In the fixed instant of immeasurable beauty which the poet, or the painter as poet, can hold forever in the palm of his eye, the breast in Intimist painting, or in the Surrealism of Chagall, is an intimation of the silence that alone can speak. These painters are also poets. They are concerned with the human image, and with the image of the breast in particular as a poetic evocation of a state of being which is a surrender to dreams, or a becoming of dreams. The poetic visions of Eluard and Chagall are perfectly synchronized; they illuminate each other. That is why I have set the jewels of the Surrealist poet against the background of Chagall's silver-winged evocation.

'Man,' says Paul Valéry, 'possesses a certain look which makes him disappear; himself and all the rest, beings, earth, and sky; and which fixes itself in time out of time.'[1] It is with such a look that I am concerned here, and with the appearance of the breast as an integral aspect of this look.

So far we have seen the breast materialize in paint and stone, to reflect the active, rather than the passive conditions of human existence. Yet the latter condition is always more heavily loaded with meaning. The dream is more potent than the reality; if there is any other reality. This is the chapter of the breast as dream.

The aestheticism of Greece, the eroticism of India, the misogyny of the middle ages, the obsessions of Fuseli, are all active conditions in which the appearance of the breast plays a positive part. But life is only a moment of physical awareness with its tail in the past, and its head in the clouds of the future. We must of necessity dream more than we can live. Life is only the splutter of a match on a dark night sandwiched between a dream of what has been, and what might be. We are no more than this. Therefore a painting which captures the quality of dreaming, of reflection, of infinity one might say, is the measure of the ultimate state of our being.

[1] Paul Eluard, *Selected Writings.* (Routledge & Kegan Paul.)

Beyond sex and sensuality the body and the breasts of a woman immersed in the waters of reverie, exist out of sexual time. There is less sex in fact than Freud imagined. Bonnard, Degas and Sickert make that perfectly clear in their private views of the passivity of women at their toilet. Like D. H. Lawrence, Beardsley or Dali, Freud was partially deceived by his own obsessions. He sought to swallow the world into the bowels of his own subjectivity. Where he personally saw only sex, he argued that the world should see only sex. I would reject Freud's excessive emphasis on the sexual instinct; it is an aspect of life, but not its entirety. Naturally, one cannot question the incontrovertible evidence that so patently exists of the validity of Freud's scheme of sexual symbolism as it manifests itself in dreams and fantasies, and also of course in the skilfully contrived surrealism of Dali. But I do suggest that one can make too much of sex, and I do most passionately believe that the greater part of free association day dreaming, and indeed of plain night-time dreaming, is less sexual, more tender, and more innocently childlike, than is generally supposed. And in spite of Freud I believe in the innocence of childhood. I am aware that he places tremendous emphasis upon the alleged sexual content of the functions and events of early childhood, and that he ascribes the formation of adult character to an early interest in certain bodily organs and their functions. Generosity we are told springs from an early fixation in oral erotic sensation; stubbornness from an arrested interest in excrement. Add to this the whole glamorous gamut of 'fecal' renunciation, 'penis' envy, and 'castration' fear, and the picture of our early years is far from pleasant. Dali, the insincere, contriving surrealist, supports this conception. Chagall does not. In Dali the conception of the breast is indissolubly linked with the vocabulary of Freudian symbolism; in Chagall its sexual content and significance is at a minimum.

It may well be, as Freud suggests, that mouth, anus, breast and genitalia are the bedrock of all that we are psychologically, or psycho-analytically, but I would still argue that the breast can have associations other than sexual ones. Sexuality may comprise the basic level of our existence, but on a different plane there is our spiritual and metaphysical identity. Both Jung and Adler suspected Freud's narrowness of outlook. Even if, unconsciously, the breast evokes images, or sensations of the pleasure we once took in being cuddled by our mothers may it not be a pure, asexual joy that is recalled? As I see it, this is the difference between the innocent conception of the breast in Chagall, and Dali's images of this member, fat with Freudian suckling.

Sex is not all. In fact, that is far from the case. Consider the nude for a moment. There is nothing so sexless as the nude. 'The view through the keyhole,' to quote Degas, far from revealing the visions of voluptuousness that schoolboys imagine, is more likely to throw back an image as sexless as Bonnard's 'Woman in the Bath' (Plate 99). The condition of pure passivity is asexual. A woman in the bath with her breasts floating like jelly-fish is hardly the stuff of desire. But it is the stuff of dreams. At her ablutions, or her toilet, a woman grows pensive; the stream of consciousness is as likely to flow from her in the bath as in bed, and I have often thought that Bonnard's water-logged, reflective nude could so well be Mrs Bloom in the throes of her soliloquy: 'and drew him down to me so he could feel my breasts all perfume . . .' What more likely vision in her mind's eye as her thoughts spin, and weave, than such a vision as Chagall has captured in his 'Lovers on a Horse' (Plate 98) . . . 'my breasts all perfume . . .' These two pictures, with their passive conception of the breast, mirror the two sides of the medal of the private view. The body from which dreams spring, and the dream itself.

Compare the floating breasts, and the soaring breasts; the real breasts, and the dream breasts, both watery, substanceless, swansdown light. Clouds. In his essay 'Women in Europe',[1] Carl Jung speaks of the 'unconsciousness and indefiniteness of the woman', and it is this very faculty which they possess for making both their bodies, and their personalities, blurred and indistinct on occasions, that is so tenderly and delicately reflected in the imagery of Bonnard, and Chagall. Spirituality quickly supersedes the physically sensual in women, a fact which few men are able (or would be willing) to realize; but Jung, with his keen sense of the mystical potentialities of personality, is well aware of this essentially feminine quality. One would not have expected the same discernment from Freud.

In the light of these comments I would like for a moment to compare the mood of the toilet with that of the dream: with the pure dreams of Chagall, not the ravaged fantasies of Dali. There will be time later to consider the appearance of the breast in the vision of the Spanish surrealist.

[1] C. G. Jung,' Women in Europe' (1927), pp. 164-88 of the *Contributions to Analytical Psychology* (London: 1928).

The auto-hypnosis which washing, combing the hair, or simply floating in the bath induces, carries the dreamer, and the artist—if he happens to be looking—like driftwood, to that other keyhole through which the soul is revealed. The painter, in taking his preliminary view through Degas' keyhole, hovers close to the other: '. . . It is not only naked bodies that we surprise through the keyhole, but naked souls. They speak to us in silence and act in immobility. It is their very immobility that speaks.'[2] Anthony Bertram's inspired extension of Degas' phrase 'the view through the keyhole', is perfectly mirrored in the ruminative aspect of Bonnard's women, as it is indeed in so many of the intimist views that Degas (Plate 100) and Sickert afford us of women at their toilet reveries. In that magical moment of maximum reflection, of 'unconsciousness' and 'indefiniteness', the body of a woman sheds the tight skin of its sensuality, relaxing into dreams and recollections, under the soothing caress of water and soap, scrubbing brush and sponge. The keys of paradise are more handy than one imagines. Under the influence of mescalin Huxley found a shining eternity in the crease of his trousers; the caress of a sponge may open the same door.

In the bath, and at her toilet, a woman's breasts spread wide like water-lilies, or hang, passively, relieved of all sensual stress. The private view is a view of the soul cleansed of desire, or the power to arouse desire. And since art is a reflection of life, the whole of life seen in the one, aesthetic aspect,[2] surrealist painters like Chagall offer an essentially innocent vision of the breast, because dreams, and waking fantasies, lack the erotic tensions of life. Only the erotic nightmare is taut and aggressive; the natural dream, even when sensual, is fluid, melting, and relatively passive.

A woman washing, or scrubbing her back, or floating in the bath, or rising light as a dove's breath in the arms of her lover, has achieved release from the gross clamourings of the flesh. She is no longer earthbound. Molly Bloom's stream of reverie, although it embraces many sensual reflections, is still sexless because random erotic fantasies, flashing like the rays of a lighthouse, without time to harden or crystallize, are in themselves substanceless. Only the carefully contrived fantasies of Dali

---

[1] Anthony Bertram *Sickert*, 1955. (Studio Books.)

[2] I am indebted to the late J. E. Barton for this reflection. In his book *Purpose and Admiration* the author defines art not as 'one aspect of life, but the whole of life seen in one aspect'.

(Plate 103), or sometimes Beardsley (Plate 102) have opacity. Like the visions of madmen they are fixed, static; images in a room forever lit by a high-powered electric lamp. They are harsh indications only of personal obsessions. On the contrary, the gentle, indistinct visions of Chagall invite us into the secret heart of their being. We can identify ourself with his dreams, just as we can participate in the mood of reverie that Bonnard and Degas communicate with such penetrating felicity. Each of these artists strikes the common chord. On the other hand, Beardsley's many-breasted fantasy is surely close to madness—sharply defined, shrill, hallucinatory. Dali's 'Spectre of Sex Appeal' (Plate 101), for all the excitement of its imagery, evokes a similar response. Anyone who is familiar with the tedious, overworked techniques of psychotic art will want to draw a comparison between Dali's obsessional style, and the meticulously rendered imagery of madness. In this respect both Beardsley and Dali represent the exception rather than the rule. Normally, we see, both literally and imaginatively, as Impressionists; a little at a time in focus, and a lot out. The obsessive definition of detail which both Beardsley and Dali employ suggests the private view of madness rather than sanity; especially when this extreme clarity of vision is coupled with a tormented personal iconography.

Psychologically, Dali's art has of course much of great interest to commend it, providing as it does a classic illustration of consciously constructed sexual fantasy. His concoctions are so obviously not dreams in the accepted sense of the term, but visions put together piece by piece as one might work out a jig-saw. Dali's fantasy is continued with all the ingenious daring of an oversexed schoolboy of genius. His pictures are hard, deliberate expressions of sexual hysteria with none of the soft, indistinct, smooth-flowing fortuitousness of the genuine dream. The fundamental concept upon which the whole edifice of Surrealist art is founded is the undirected expression of the unconscious, in words or pictorial images, beyond the exercise of all reason, or of any conscious control on the part of the artist, or the writer. It was André Breton, leader of the Surrealist movement, who set these terms of reference in the first Surrealist Manifesto of 1924. Dali does not fulfil these conditions, whereas Chagall does. One can feel the dreams flowing free and uncontrolled from his mind's eye.

We are now faced with a group of private views, in each of which the breast figures prominently. There is the reflective, asexual view of the toilet, the lightly flavoured sexuality of the reverie and the authentic dream—as in the case of Chagall—and the crystalline, flint-sharp hallucinations of near madness, or simulated madness. Although Beardsley's fever of breasts is admittedly one of the artist's illustrations for Ben Jonson's *Volpone*, it stands as a classic example of the psychopathological erotic fantasy; a private view with little relation to the norm of the collective unconscious. In assessing Beardsley's eroticism one must of course bear in mind the degree to which this was aggravated by tuberculosis from which the artist died in 1898, the year in which his five illustrations for *Volpone* were produced. Beardsley had originally planned twenty-four illustrations, of which the illustration here is one.

Somewhere between the momentary experiences of life, and the infinite world of dreams, which is our true and only substance, there exists a point of visual crystallization, tender and fragile, in which we may apprehend eternity. Where this vision is demented, or warped, the personality has failed to establish contact with the stream of timelessness, and finds itself locked, as do Beardsley or Dali, in the fixed 'now' of delusion. The mysticism of Chagall, Molly Bloom's smoothly flowing river of reflections, Eluard's fragrant evocations, can show us the image of our longing to recapture, to re-create, the gentler patterns of experience and being that alone can set us free. It is the transcendent potentialities of experience that are so magnificently symbolized in Chagall's vision of the breast; the clay-footed, and tormented cravings of the corruptible body that Dali—and Beardsley—present in their visions of frustration and putrefaction are earth-bound. The mystical reclamation of the spirit of childhood and youth, out of time, is the essence of Chagall's vision. For if we are anything at all, anything that is, which matters, then we are spirit. As flesh, we are only agony and dust. The longing to transcend the body, to enter into the healing stream of timelessness, illuminates the breasts, and the passive faces of the women in the art of Bonnard and Degas. The visions of Chagall suggest that our deepest yearnings are linked with the ache to escape from just such fantasies and obsessions as those which hold both Beardsley and Dali prisoners in time; in sexual time. Freud is right for them, but not for Chagall. Sigmund is the measure of the flesh, but not of the soul.

Let Eluard speak of this miraculous other world of the soul in which lie hidden the mystic jewels of our real identity:

'There was a time when I seemed to understand nothing. My chains floated on water. All my desires are born of my dreams. And I have proven my love with words. To what fantastic creatures have I entrusted myself, in what dolorous and ravishing world has my imagination enclosed me? I am sure of having been loved in the most mysterious domains, my own. The language of my love does not belong to human language, my human body does not touch the flesh of my love. My amorous imagination has always been constant and high enough so that nothing could attempt to convince me of error.'

(From *At the Window*, 1926.[1])

The language of my love does not belong to human language, my human body does not touch the flesh of my love. Could one find a more perfect literary complement for Chagall's aesthetic vision? I think not. If we have any hope of salvation it is vested in this world alone. The Freudian view is a vision of the damned.

★

Dali once said that the only difference between himself and a madman is that he is not mad. I will not debate the issue. The 'paranoiac visions' of the painter at least afford a clear idea of what it means to be imprisoned in the labyrinths of the Freudian limbo. How close this condition is to madness I would not know, but certainly Dali's sexual fantasy must stretch the limits of neurosis pretty close to the frontiers of full-blown psychosis. The use of stuffed sacks to symbolize the breasts in 'The Spectre of Sex Appeal' clearly indicates the existence of repressed sexual material. Dali's private view is thus limited by the very nature of his psychoneurosis. It has no flow, or flexibility. The artist is a prisoner, whereas Chagall is a free man. Dali cannot break out of the tight framework of his 'paranoiac vision', and although he is anxious to associate himself with madness and yet claim simultaneously a clean bill of health, so acute are the symptoms of dissociation which he continuously manifests in his painting, that one must seriously doubt his claim. The conversion hysteria which is demonstrated by his transposition of breasts into sacks of debris—unthinkable in the iconography of Chagall—supports his admitted fascination for decay and putrefaction. Dali

---

[1] Paul Eluard, *Selected Writings.* (Routledge & Kegan Paul.)

frequently distorts his representation of the breast. Sometimes it is shown with the nipples sprouting cancerous tentacles, or in process of being crushed, all of which suggests, as do the stuffed bags, a repressed longing to defile and desecrate the most beautiful feature of a woman's body. Why? Obviously I am not qualified to offer a professional explanation, but common sense, and a working knowledge of morbid psychology, make feasible a tolerable amateur explanation. It seems to me that Dali's frequent attacks on the female breast, and his obsession with its distortion, indicate in the best Freudian sense, the existence in his unconscious of some severe childhood trauma in which the breast figured as an image of shock, or frustration. In what circumstances, I naturally could not say; but there are many possibilities; the sight of illicit love-making perhaps, and the kindling of resentment and jealousy in an infant's heart, or the plain, sudden withdrawal of the breast from an infant. Particularly if the child was consistently denied this pleasure. Whatever the circumstances, however, Dali has frequently taken his revenge upon the offending member. The conversion of the breasts into sacks filled with rubbish, or debris, symbolizes this hatred, and the desire to enjoy, and to gloat over, at least symbolically, a vision of breasts in ruin and decay. The presence of the little boy in the right-hand corner of the picture, offers I think further support for my interpretation since it is patently an autobiographical image.

But there are almost certainly clues to the nature of the trauma which the infant Dali may have suffered, in his own 'explanation' of The Spectre of Sex Appeal. In his study by Dali,[1] James Thrall Soby quotes the artist as saying:

> ' "I am very proud of having predicted in 1928, at the height of the cult for functional and practical anatomy, in the midst of the most shocking scepticism, *the imminence of the round and salivary muscles of Mae West, viscous and terrible with hidden biological meanings.* Today I announce that all the new sexual allure of women will come from the possible utilization of their capacities and resources as ghosts, that is to say from their charnel and luminous decomposition." He added (writes Soby) that the woman with sex appeal would henceforth be demountable as the figure in "The Spectre of Sex Appeal" quite clearly is, *so that she could satisfy her profound*

[1] James Thrall Soby, *Salvador Dali.* (Museum of Modern Art, New York.)

exhibitionism by detaching sections of her anatomy and passing them around to be admired separately.'

I have myself italicized portions of the above because I think these contain the genuine clues for which we are looking. Discounting the sheer writing for effect, there is first of all the ironic and loathing references to the breast as 'salivary muscles', 'viscous and terrible with hidden biological meanings' and, perhaps most revealing of all, the satirical and accusing description of the sexual exhibitionism of the central figure in the artist's fantasy. May this not be an attack upon the cheapening to which a woman of flirtatious disposition is subject? I will leave the reader to infer any further conclusions.

Whatever the answer, Dali's 'paranoiac visions' clearly demonstrate that the Freudian situation is fraught with stress and tension; with amours that have gone astray, and hatreds that drag in their wake the heavy chains of remorse and shame. Nothing is straightforward; all is double-think—double-talk. Hidden meanings, ambivalent parent fixations, symbols of indescribable horror replace the clear imagery of the innocent soul, and the crystal visions that poets have preserved in the teeth of Freud's apocalypse of repression and symbolic guilt. There is no doubt that our lives are lived partly on the Freudian level, but that is not the whole of life. There is also our longing, and our struggle to regain the innocence that we have lost, and that we re-approach in reveries and dreams. I cannot accept the concept of 'original sin', but I do believe in man's fall from innocence. This belief has no religious significance, but then neither has the evil which springs from our lost innocence. Let me explain. Not long ago a friend suggested a likely answer to the whole problem of human wickedness, and of the suffering and grief that stems both from the evil of our own actions, and that which *appears* to arise from sources and factors over which we have no control and for which consequently it would seem that we have no responsibility. This is not so. All evil, ugliness, disease of mind, and body, emanates directly from those actions committed either by us, or on our behalf, by our ancestors. In the course of my conversation with this friend I had raised the question of how one could reconcile the concept of a loving god with the sufferings of illness, and disease that attack, alike, the guilty and the apparently innocent. How for instance does one reconcile the visitation of illness and disease upon little children, with the idea of a loving creator? Or

139

the visitation of madness? His answer was of the simplest kind. Evil, sickness, disease, insanity, he argued, spring from centuries of *wrong thinking, and wrong living.* We have free will; that is the creator's supreme gift. It is our choice whether we think and act, ill or well. By virtue of this argument we can see that every form of psychological, physiological, and even genetic disease, may well be the result of wrong thinking, and wrong living, somewhere along the line of our evolution. We are all guilty; no one is innocent, least of all the unborn for they inherit our guilt by proxy. We all flow from the common stream.

Dali's fantasy, and indeed the whole Freudian scheme, can be explained in the light of this hypothesis. When the unconscious, out of shame, or guilt, or fear, erects its structure of symbolic imagery to carry the burden of our repressions and complexes—we cannot think straight even in our fantasies—that in itself is the proof, and the indictment, of the wrong thinking and the wrong living that has brought into being the need for such a terrible defence mechanism. Let us consider an example of psychological wrong thinking, in which the breast figures prominently. When Dali envisaged 'The Resurrection of the Flesh' (Plate 103) he perpetuated the tradition of wrong thinking. It is not the resurrection of the flesh, with all its cupidities, and lusts, that we should yearn for, but the redemption of the soul which has no form, or shape. Consider the gross breasts of the female figure rising from the swamp of Dali's resurrection, her nakedness pouring with the spoils and trinkets of greed, while the still putrescent figure of a man struggles to clutch at her flesh in the first requickening of his mortal lust. The attitude is a classic example of wrong thinking. It is an attitude of mind which conceives sex as an end, and not as a means to another, more absolute end. On the other hand the right thinking of Hindu eroticism approaches the state of sexuality as the means to an end; as the gateway through which we may recover union with God, with Brahma, and through this union reclaim, at last, the peaceful pastures and the simple visions of our lost innocence. Of such an innocent return to grace the Adamite, Hieronymus Bosch, dreamed in his 'Garden of Earthly Delights'. Apart from the many stock medieval symbols which the central panel contains, the Millennium is primarily a vision of paradise regained. A dream of the triumph of love, rising in all its shining purity from the ashes of sensuality. It is a first vision of the world; a vision of children and saints, for whom there is only the wonder and the perfection of creation. Beyond the need for double-think and double-talk; beyond the cross of Freud and psycho-analysis, and the symbolic images of repression, and guilt, and fear, rise the fireflies of the poet's eye, of the child's eye, and the saint's, and the prostitute's eye. She who is rejected and denied, even in her humanity, as Christ Himself was rejected and denied. These are the lambs of God. The child, the saint, the prostitute and the poet (and the painter-poets, such as Bosch and Chagall) are the true visionaries. They alone see purely. The prostitute in her degradation and martyrdom is already cleansed of the world. The child and the saint are beyond taint. And the poet, consciously striving, for our sake, to reclaim the visions of innocence that we lose in the shadowy vale of the world's evil, is our conscience, and our saviour.

The poet's eye is the brook in which the roots of memory are washed clean.

Listening to the band in Hyde Park, one summer afternoon, watching the gently bowed heads, and the tenderly uplifted faces set like onyx silhouettes against the pools of opalescent sunlight that broke open the doors of the shadows, I saw a vision of mankind longing to be free from the rack of the world; yearning to soar, and rise, on the breasts of reverie, into paradise.

The private view that Bonnard, and Degas and Chagall offer us, is only another reflection of the common longing to find again the images of innocence upon which, in the words of Camus, our 'whole being opened for the first time'. In the eye of these artists the dreaming breasts of women are a symbol of the return.

★

INDEX

INDEX